TRUE STORIES OF RIVERSIDE AND THE INLAND EMPIRE

TRUE STORIES OF RIVERSIDE AND THE INLAND EMPIRE

HAL DURIAN

THE History PRESS

Published by The History Press
Charleston, SC 29403
www.historypress.net

First published 2013

Manufactured in the United States

ISBN 978.1.60949.773.6

Library of Congress CIP data applied for.

This book is dedicated to Riverside County judges John G. Gabbert and Victor Miceli.

Contents

Acknowledgements

There are so many individuals and organizations that have contributed to this book that I am sure I will offend some by omission.

The Riverside Public Library has been most helpful for the seven years that the column "Riverside Recollections" was printed in the *Riverside Press-Enterprise*. Ruth McCormick, reference librarian, deserves more thanks than I can express.

Across the street from the library is the Riverside Metropolitan Museum. Kevin Hallaran of the museum has consistently gone out of his way to assist me.

My alma mater, the University of California–Riverside (UCR), has helped greatly. Howard P. Parks and Reverend Glen Wenzel, both Riverside authors of local history, have provided both encouragement and photos.

Jerry Roberts of The History Press deserves credit, or blame, for proposing this project. Nels Jensen of the *Riverside Press-Enterprise* was kind enough to permit the reprinting of the columns included in this work. My son and daughter-in-law, Matthew and Norma Durian, employed some computer wizardry to save the day.

Fred Bauman, a photographer with more than forty years of experience, graciously granted permission for use of the incredible cover photo. That photo is probably the most beautiful one ever taken of downtown Riverside.

Individuals who deserve recognition for their guidance and assistance along the way in my research must be led by Riverside's most distinguished person, Judge John Gabbert (retired). No other living person is represented

John G. Gabbert Judicial Plaza honors the long-serving judge in downtown Riverside. *Photo by the author.*

by a monument on Main Street in Riverside. At this writing, Judge Gabbert is 103, and his memory is sharp.

Joan Hall, author of eight books on Riverside, has been most generous in assisting me. Steve Lech of the Riverside Historical Society has also been most helpful. Bill T. Mills and his friends at American Legion Post No. 289 have been most supportive of this fellow legionnaire. Frank Tourlay, the expert on Camp Anza, has gone out of his way to assist me. Lew Vanderzyl knows Riverside and its schools better than almost anyone else. His uncle, Bob Vanderzyl, was my tennis coach at Riverside's Poly High in the 1950s.

The following folks either suggested or provided specific information for individual columns that appear in this book: John Adams, Suzanne Armas, Al Bellavia, Dan Bernstein, James Bryant, Bill Cooper, Nancy Cox, Courtney Donowho of the Riverside County Sheriff's Department, Melba Dunlap, Riverside police officer Mike Eveland, Louise Felicetta, Dick Garton, Kevin Hallaran of the Riverside Metropolitan Museum, Beatty Elementary School principal Debbie Ausman Haskins, Jessica Herdina, the Heritage Room and the Reference Desk of the Corona Public Library, Kim Jarrell Johnson, Jon Lue, Tom Mazzetti, Ruth McCormick, Dr. Vince Moses, Cindie Perry, Ron Pidot, Lynne and Ron Preston, Christine Reifel, Judge Elwood Rich, Steve Spiller of the Mission Inn, Riverside police captain Bill St. Marie, Dennis Timmons, Carolyn Ulrich, Bob "Fritz" Umphress, Dusty Williams and Mark Yeager.

Introduction

For seven years, I was fortunate to write about the history of Riverside and its neighboring cities and towns for one of the nation's finest medium-sized newspapers. The *Riverside Press-Enterprise* won the Pulitzer Prize for investigative reporting in 1968, and it carried two cases to the U.S. Supreme Court on freedom of the press and won both of them. I am proud to have written for one of the land's finest newspapers.

My association with the newspaper goes back to 1950. From 1950 to 1952, I was a carrier boy for the *Riverside Daily Press*, the predecessor of the *P-E*. Therefore, I have worked at the newspaper, off and on, for nearly sixty-five years. That figure includes more than half a century "off." The association was rewarding.

If I had a devoted reader who read all of my columns from 2005 through 2012, he or she would still find something new in this book. Some of these columns weren't printed in the *P-E* for one reason or another.

I hope that this book will be of interest to readers of Southern California history. While the focus is on Riverside County, the stories spill over into contiguous counties, mostly San Bernardino, the largest county in area in the lower forty-eight states. Riverside and San Bernardino Counties, containing more than 4 million people, have earned the gaudy nickname the "Inland Empire." I'm pleased to pass on these stories to a new generation.

Part I
Early Times

Don Pedro Fages Was First

Most residents of the Riverside area believe that Don Juan Bautista de Anza was the first European to pass through the environs of Riverside. The historical record indicates that Lieutenant Pedro Fages (sometimes spelled Faxes or even Faces) passed through here in 1772, two years before De Anza. Lieutenant Fages rode through the land that later became Riverside before passing through the Cajon Pass on his way to the Presidio at Monterey.

According to his diary, Pedro Fages was not primarily an explorer. Instead, his main mission was to search and capture deserters from the Spanish army. There was some reason to desert the Spanish army of 1770, as seen by the record of the ship that carried Fages and his troops from La Paz in what is today's Baja California, Mexico, to San Diego in 1769. That voyage of less than 1,300 miles took the lives of almost one-third of the soldiers and crewmen aboard the Spanish vessel *San Carlos*. These deaths were caused by scurvy, lack of fresh water and resulting illness. That disastrous voyage took 110 days due to uncooperative winds, poor navigation and opposing currents.

Pedro Fages was in command of the reduced garrison that landed at San Diego. In his diary, he reported that the male Indians there ran around completely naked, while females covered their midsections. Some of the Indians were hostile to the Spaniards, so Fages demonstrated the military superiority of the Spanish army in a very clever way. He placed the thick leather army breastplate, worn as part of the soldier's uniform, on a tree and invited the Indian braves to shoot their arrows at it. The Indians saw the heavy leather resist almost all of the arrows that hit the regulation army breastplate. This demonstration discouraged most Indians from attacking the Spaniards.

Fages came from the Catalan section of Spain, the area around Barcelona. He was popular with his troops and with children, but surprisingly, he had a feud with the saintly Father Junipero Serra, founder of the California missions. Perhaps it was not unusual that a military commander and a Spanish priest would disagree on how to deal with the Indians they encountered.

Pedro Fages must have been a most able commander. He was promoted from lieutenant to captain and later to lieutenant colonel. For a time, he served as governor of Alta California, with headquarters in Monterey. Along the way, he acquired the nickname "El Oso" (the Bear), because of the bear hunts he made to supply his troops with meat.

In 1780, Pedro Fages married Dona Eulalia Callis, a woman born in Spain but then residing in Mexico City. She was called the first woman of quality to make her home in Alta California.

Fages died in 1794 at a time when George Washington was president of the United States. Fages is remembered as a soldier, explorer and governor of both Alta and Baja California from 1782 to 1791.

While serving as governor, Fages made important land grants, including one to Antonio Yorba and Pablo Peralta that included much of today's Orange County. Another land grant executed by Fages was made to Manuel Nieto and included the land between the San Gabriel River and the Santa Ana River.

Fages was depicted as one of the characters in the 1955 film *Seven Cities of Gold*. The Chilean novelist Isabel Allende mentions both Fages and his wife in her 2005 novel *Zorro*.

THE EXCITING LIFE OF BENJAMIN WILSON

Before Louis Rubidoux came to California, Benjamin Wilson, then known as Don Benito, had married into the famous Yorba landowning family and had become one of the great landowners of Southern California.

Wilson was respected by most of the Indian tribes of the area, but renegade groups of Indians stole livestock and caused fear and unrest in California in the 1840s. Wilson led armed parties to attack the Indian outlaws, and in one venture, Wilson was shot in the shoulder by a poisoned arrow. Wilson's faithful Indian companion sucked the poison out of the wound, and Wilson recovered from an injury that could have been fatal.

Part of Wilson's landholding was the 1.5 leagues (six thousand acres) known as Jurupa Rancho, situated on both sides of the Santa Ana River. Later, he sold part of the Jurupa Rancho to Lorenzo Trujillo, who was a leader of the Agua Mansa community. Another portion of land was sold to Isaac Williams, owner of the Chino Rancho. In 1848, Wilson sold the remaining half of his Jurupa Rancho to Louis Rubidoux, a name familiar to all Riverside residents.

During the war with Mexico (1846–48), California was split between the Californios loyal to Mexico and the supporters of the United States. In the so-called Battle of Chino—actually more of a skirmish—Wilson, Rubidoux and Williams of Chino (all supporters of the United States) were taken prisoner. Their situation was desperate. All three of these men could have been found guilty of treason against Mexico and shot. Fortunately, the three men were later released by their captors.

California became independent of Mexico in 1848 and was made a state in 1850 when Ben Wilson ran as a Know-Nothing candidate for the California legislature. The Know-Nothing Party was a minor party opposed to immigration into the United States. In his race for state senator, Wilson lost in San Bernardino County but carried the more populous Los Angeles County and was elected to the California state senate. Riverside County was not created until 1893.

Wilson bought and sold land, amassing a fortune. He chose to live in the area now known as San Marino near Pasadena. The mountain now famous for its observatories, Mount Wilson, was named for Benjamin Wilson. He lived a long, full life. At one point, he was elected mayor of Los Angeles, either the first or second Anglo mayor of that city, depending on which source one reads.

Wilson's family grew and developed roots in San Marino and adjacent Pasadena. One of Wilson's grandsons achieved fame as General George S. Patton Jr., the daring leader of the Third Army in World War II. Also in that war, a Liberty ship was launched with the name *Benjamin D. Wilson*. His granddaughter, Anne W. Patton, sister of the general, was given the honor of christening the new vessel.

Benjamin Wilson's career seemed to be successful despite some setbacks under Mexican rule of California. Possibly General Patton inherited some of his daring and fighting spirit from his grandfather, the old Indian fighter and California politician.

DISAPPEARED WITHOUT A TRACE

Michigan had Jimmy Hoffa. New York had Judge Crater. And Riverside had Tom Cover. Each of these men disappeared without a trace, and the fate and whereabouts of their remains are unknown to this day.

Tom Cover was a miner and explorer of the West. He lived in Montana in the late 1860s where he was part of a vigilante group. In the late 1860s, he moved to the area we now call Riverside. He worked in the silk growing ranch that existed here before John North founded and surveyed Riverside.

Cover's gold fever, begun in Montana, continued in California, and he searched for gold in the hills and ravines near what is today the Salton Sea. Cover disappeared at a time when he was only a mile or so away from his prospecting partner. Cover had gone in a separate direction from his friend, and in a short time, his disappearance was complete.

Years later, bones were found in the general area where the men had been, but there was no indication that the bones had belonged to Tom Cover. Naturally, several theories were developed as to the fate of the experienced outdoorsman and miner. One theory held that Cover had fled and hidden from friend and foe alike. He might have traveled to South America to explore gold mining possibilities there. Another theory maintained that some of Cover's enemies from the vigilante days in Montana were in the area, and they could have spirited him away and later killed him.

In our time, it is much more difficult to disappear completely and take on a new identity. Fingerprints, DNA analysis and photo identity cards all serve to pinpoint a person's identity, living or dead.

Tom Cover came to Riverside months or years before Judge North and his colonists from the east established the model colony they called Riverside. Cover worked at the silk ranch and bought acreage on which he built a fine home on the southwest corner of today's Palm and Jurupa Avenues. That home is gone today, but Cover Street, named for Tom Cover, is located on land formerly owned by the miner and adventurer a few yards south of the corner lot where the Cover home once stood. It seems that history often leaves its traces, often as place names, even as the physical and economic landscapes change. Still, Tom Cover disappeared without a trace, and his fate remains a mystery.

Lorenzo and La Placita

La Placita (or "small square") was a little community on the south side of the Santa Ana River that began about 1845. Its twin community on the north side of the river was known as Agua Mansa, gentle water. But the water was not always so gentle. Both settlements were almost totally destroyed by the disastrous flood of 1862, and there were efforts to rebuild, mostly on the La Placita side of the river.

In the old days of Riverside, founded in 1870, La Placita was called Spanish Town, and North Orange Street, which led to La Placita, was known as Spanish Town Drive. Probably the leading citizen of La Placita was Lorenzo Trujillo, a Pueblo Indian born in what is today New Mexico in 1795. At the time of Lorenzo's birth, the area was under the Spanish flag. In the 1820s, it became part of Mexico, and in 1848, it became U.S. territory by virtue of the Treaty of Guadalupe-Hidalgo that ended the war with Mexico.

Lorenzo Trujillo lived to serve under all three flags. In his youth, he was a traveling peddler who went from village to village selling his wares. He was called a "Genizaro," an Indian who had taken to the white man's ways. He served as a scout for the forces of Spain and moved west with the Rowland-Workman Party in 1841.

In Lorenzo's most memorable adventure, he became assistant to Benjamin Wilson, an owner of huge tracts of land stretching from Pasadena to Redlands of today. The two men pursued Indian horse thieves, and Wilson was shot in the shoulder by an arrow that had been dipped in poison. Lorenzo sucked the poison out of the wound and saved Wilson's life.

Settling in La Placita, Lorenzo became the most respected citizen and a spokesman for the community because of his experience, his travels and his known honesty. He had a wife and several brothers who also resided in La Placita. The esteem that Lorenzo enjoyed is shown by the name given to the village. Jane Davies Gunther, in her book *Riverside County Place Names*, wrote that the village was known as "La Placita de los Trujillos" in honor of Lorenzo and his family.

All traces of La Placita are gone now, but an adobe building lasted until recent years when rain, neglect and old age caused its walls to crumble. The building in the 1920s enjoyed a colorful, even humorous series of events. Riverside County, formed in 1893, shared a border with San Bernardino County that ran through La Placita and very near the old adobe. A newer building close to the Trujillo adobe served as a bar, gambling casino and site of other illegal activities.

In the 1920s, prohibition was the law of the land, and police and county sheriff's deputies were drawn to the tavern. It was situated almost exactly on the county line, and when Riverside lawmen came, the bartender would insist that his place was in San Bernardino County and vice versa when San Bernardino officials arrived. This dodge worked for a while, apparently. Today's lawmen have statewide jurisdiction, so the scheme would not succeed.

Archaeologists have found a rich trove of artifacts from La Placita and Agua Mansa. These items are now in the possession of the anthropology department of Riverside's UCR.

Leading citizen Lorenzo Trujillo died in 1855. His many descendants include Suzanne Armas of Riverside.

RIVERSIDE FOUNDER BUILT OTHER CITIES

John W. North was born in Rensselaer County, New York, in 1815. North grew up in an idealistic family who were against slavery. He moved west to the territory of Minnesota, where he was one of the founders of the University of Minnesota and the town of Northfield, named for its founder. He is even credited with being one of the founders of Minneapolis.

The Republican Party was born in the 1850s, and North was one of Minnesota's most active members. He was on the delegation that formally announced to Abraham Lincoln that he was the GOP nominee for president in 1860. After taking office, President Lincoln named North to the position of surveyor general of the Nevada Territory. He later became a judge in Nevada and was active in writing a constitution for that state.

After the Civil War, North set up a business in Knoxville, Tennessee. There he saved a black man from being killed by a lynch mob.

John North, founder of Riverside, was an appointee of Abraham Lincoln and founded towns in two states. *Courtesy of Riverside Metropolitan Museum.*

Back in the Midwest, North organized a group of friends, each of whom contributed $1,000 to buy land in California. North favored acreage in the area that is now Pasadena. Later, he and his associates settled on the area that became Riverside. North touted this land as a "Colony for California."

North's group purchased 8,600 acres from an ill-fated silk growing colony in the area east of the Santa Ana River. It was a dry, dusty plain, but there was a source of water nearby. The visionary North saw a bright future for the area that became Riverside. He was always restless, and his colonizing days did not end with Riverside. He went on to establish Oleander, now a part of Fresno.

A lawyer by profession, North finally settled in San Francisco, where he had a successful practice. He was called back to Riverside in 1883 when he was honored as the city's founder. He made a speech at the Citrus Fair that was held in Riverside.

North died in 1890 at age seventy-five. John North High School on Chicago Avenue is named for this dynamic humanitarian of many interests. Also named for North is the small park situated between two railroad stations located between University and Mission Inn Avenues. North's Riverside home once stood on this park site.

EARLY RIVERSIDE'S ODD COUPLE

This portrait of Eliza Tibbetts was taken by Edouart & Son of 121 Spring Street, Los Angeles. *Courtesy of Riverside Metropolitan Museum.*

Most Riversiders have heard the story of Eliza Tibbets receiving orange trees from Bahia, Brazil, by way of Washington, D.C., and watering them with dishwater. Fewer people know that Eliza and Luther Tibbets were most unusual individuals. Some would say that they were true eccentrics. However, even eccentrics can make lasting contributions to society.

Eliza Tibbets was born in Ohio in 1873 and became the third wife of Luther Calvin Tibbets. His first two wives had died. Luther acquired 160 acres in 1870 between Arlington and Jurupa Avenues and farmed wheat. Eliza had lived in Washington, where her neighbor was William Saunders of the U.S. Department of Agriculture. Saunders's duties included importing plants for experimental planting. Eliza persuaded Saunders to send her a few navel orange trees, originally from Bahia, Brazil.

When the trees arrived, the Tibbets were able to secure the aid of neighbors who were nurserymen. These friendly neighbors were able to coach them on how to protect and nurture their exotic orange trees. Riverside's climate and soil were ideal for the navel orange trees. Soon, neighbors were asking for buds or cuttings from the trees, and a multimillion-dollar business was born.

Eliza's main interest in life was not the orange trees, though. She was deeply involved in religion, especially spiritualism. She would hold séances and go into trances in which an Indian girl would speak to her, she later reported. Eliza bore a striking resemblance to a contemporary, Queen Victoria of Britain. To enhance the similarity, Eliza wore clothing similar to that of Victoria.

Luther Tibbets was perhaps even more eccentric. He wore a hat with a woman's veil that he could pull over his face in order to shield his eyes from the sun or conceal his identity. He was stubborn and cantankerous and sued John North, founder of Riverside, and others over water rights. He rarely won his lawsuits, but he was very well known in the courtrooms of the day. Luther's penchants for lawsuits and unwise business deals cost him his land and his fortune. He died almost penniless in Riverside County Hospital in 1902. Eliza had died in 1898 in the home of spiritualist friends in Santa Barbara.

This dancer-like sculpture of Eliza Tibbets in a flowing gown, located on Main Street Mall in Riverside, contrasts with the rather heavyset Eliza in life. *Photo by the author.*

In their last days together, living in near poverty, Eliza and Luther could sit on their front porch and see, in all directions, orange groves that had descended from their early plantings.

Poor Daisy and the First La Cadena Bridge

For the first few years of Riverside's history, beginning in 1870, settlers had to get their water for household use from the Santa Ana River by using barrels and jars. In the dry months, it appears that the pioneers bathed less frequently.

There were no bridges across the Santa Ana River in those early days. The way to go from Riverside to Colton and on to San Bernardino, then the county seat, was to ford the river. In dry months, that was fairly easily done. In wet times, people either used a rowboat or stayed home.

Eliza and Luther Tibbets took a trip with their ten-year-old granddaughter, Daisy Summons, to Colton. Colton in 1873 had a population of fourteen, and a photo of thirteen of them is housed in today's Colton Library. One woman was otherwise occupied and could not make the photo shoot.

Luther was urging his horse on as it went into the Santa Ana River when the wagon tipped over, and poor Daisy drowned. The accident took place in 1878, eight years after Riverside's Mile Square had been surveyed and the first homes and stores had been built. The death of young Daisy spurred construction of the first bridge across the Santa Ana River at the street today known as La Cadena Drive. That road has had several names through its almost 140 years of existence. In Colton, it was Eighth Street, and for many years, the road was known as Colton Avenue in Riverside.

Sometime before 1930, Riverside and Colton agreed that the road would be known as La Cadena Drive. This road was part of the state highway beginning about that time. Looking from north to south, La Cadena Drive begins at San Bernardino Valley College and proceeds through Colton under the east–west railroad tracks and on to Riverside County. In Riverside, the early Colton Avenue turned right on what is today Strong Street. A photo from 1913 shows the Strong Street home that later belonged to William Boyd, Hollywood's Hopalong Cassidy. This photo confirms that the Strong Street of today was once part of Colton Avenue, the highway link between Riverside and San Bernardino.

In later years, the state highway, heading south from Colton, emptied into Russell Street. The highway continued to Main Street and, running stop-go, turned onto Market Street, which became Magnolia Avenue and led to Corona and the beach cities.

Looking at Russell Street today, it is hard to believe that it was part of the major highway between Colton and the beach cities. This arrangement continued until sometime in the mid-1950s, when the present 15 Freeway was built as part of the interstate highway program. That 15 Freeway chewed up much of the old La Cadena Drive, but the western part of La Cadena appears to be little changed from the 1850s. And curiously, there are in Riverside County between the San Bernardino County line and the new Highway 60 interchange two La Cadena Drives, one west of the freeway and the other east of it.

La Cadena means "the chain" in Spanish, and for decades, La Cadena Drive was the main highway that linked the cities of San Bernardino, Colton and Riverside.

The Blue and the Gray in Riverside

Riverside was formed in 1870 and was incorporated as a city in 1883. Many former Civil War soldiers made their way west and played important roles in developing inland Southern California.

Because of his family name, James H. Blue of Mississippi is the one who caught my eye. Mr. Blue fought wearing the gray uniform of the Confederacy against the Union army, which wore blue. It was a colorful but confusing war. Blue served on the staff of Confederate general Albert Sydney Johnston and was by the general's side when he was killed at the Battle of Shiloh in April 1862. Blue is buried at Evergreen Cemetery, Riverside.

James M. Drake was a Confederate soldier from Alabama who traveled west to Riverside, where he became the city treasurer.

In nearby Colton, Noel Davenport became one of the leading citizens of that town. He was born in Mobile, Alabama, in 1847, and he served in the Army of the Confederate States, apparently without great distinction. After the War Between the States, Davenport went first to San Francisco and then to San Diego. He worked as a surveyor for the San Diego and San Bernardino Railway. In 1876, he joined with A.M. Hathaway to form a general merchandise store in Colton. He also built one of the first large homes in Colton, on West G Street.

Davenport became the first notary public in Colton. His past rebellion forgotten, he was postmaster of Colton from 1881 to 1885. With an affinity for government service, he served as city clerk of Colton. Other members of his family were prominent in Colton life, public and private.

What was the reaction from the large number of Union army veterans to the fewer former Confederate soldiers, men who had faced one another on the field of battle just a few years earlier? According to a report by Elmer W. Holmes in his 1912 *History of Riverside County*, the former enemies generally got along well. He wrote, "Sincerity, tested on many a bloody battlefield, has melted the prejudices of the past and fused the men of that era into the truest of Americans."

GOTHIC CHURCH DATES TO EARLY DAYS

Templo Ebenezer dates to 1887 and is the oldest known church in Riverside. *Photo by the author.*

The Templo Ebenezer, located on Riverside's East Side, may be the oldest continuously operating church in Riverside. I have not found an older church at least. This church was built in 1887 when Riverside was only seventeen years old.

The church was built of wood frame and clapboard finish and is in the Gothic style, with stained-glass windows. At first glance, the church reminds the viewer of the famous painting *American Gothic* by Grant Wood. In its 123 years of existence, the small white church has housed Free Methodists, Southern Baptists, Pentecostals, Sons of God and other congregations.

Today, the Templo Ebenezer is home to the Pentecostal Church of Christ, with a congregation of about 150 members. The church holds three services on Sunday mornings, and the primary language used in the services is Spanish, although the 9:45 a.m. service I attended was bilingual (English/Spanish).

One of the first things a visitor notices is the youthful nature of people in attendance. Many mainline Protestant churches are facing aging congregations and declining attendance on Sunday mornings. Not so with Templo Ebenezer. There is an enthusiastic female youth minister named Mabel Vega and a lively band to encourage youth participation. The minister in charge is Pastor Ernesto Ambriz, and he is assisted by his wife, Jeanette. She directs popular services for women—services that, in Pentecostal style, often become very emotional.

It is ironic that such an old church, probably the oldest church in Riverside, should have such a youthful congregation. In my morning of attendance, there were more teenagers present than people of any other age group. Such a youthful membership promises future success for growth of the congregation.

The world has changed many times since the small white Gothic church was built. It was built in White's Addition, one of the first subdivisions added to the Mile Square, or original layout of Riverside, designed by founder John W. North.

The church is now located near the edge of an industrial area where there are several scrap metal businesses. Sixth Street, east of the railroad tracks, is a narrow street, but somehow those in attendance at the Templo Ebenezer find parking spaces. To encourage the youthful congregation, the church offers music lessons and sports activities. There are Sunday school classes for children. The interior of the church is marked by signs of a spiritual nature, almost all in Spanish. The service I attended was directed by Pastor Ambriz. It was Bible-based and delivered in bilingual form.

This old but well-maintained church is located at 2921 Sixth Street, between Commerce Street and Park Avenue. Visitors who wish to see the church will be as welcome as I was. The first Sunday service begins at 9:45 a.m. The church building has been designated Riverside Cultural Heritage Landmark no. 95.

Universalist-Unitarian Church Dates to 1891

The Universalist-Unitarian Church, in the same block as the Riverside Public Library at Mission Inn Avenue and Lemon Street, is the oldest church of its denomination west of the Rocky Mountains. The church was built in 1891 of red sandstone from Flagstaff, Arizona. It was designed by A.C. Willard and built for $25,000. The church has a medieval look, and its buttresses and its imposing crenellated tower reach fifty feet into the air.

There was a time in the late 1940s when plans were being made to construct the present downtown library, and someone suggested the purchase and demolition of the red sandstone church to clear the entire city block for library usage. Fortunately for us today, no agreement could be reached on a price for the church and its adjacent office and classroom

The Unitarian Church, as seen in 1908. *Courtesy of Riverside Metropolitan Museum.*

The renamed Universalist Unitarian Church in a twenty-first-century snapshot. *Photo by the author.*

building. The church was saved. Its future was further ensured when a group of city planners and artists was hired to consult on the library project. The group told the Riverside City Council that it would be a crime to destroy the architectural gem.

The first minister of the Riverside Universalist Church, then called All Saints Universalist Church, was George H. Deere. He became the most prominent leader in the small town of Riverside in the period of 1881–90. He served as president of the school board and the Riverside Library Board and served on the county board of education.

Today, Riverside Universalist Unitarian Church has an active membership of 130 and an average Sunday attendance of 85. It calls itself the "Uncommon Denomination." The church's members are notably active in political and social causes.

The church proudly welcomes all races, genders and people of any sexual preference. The church is proud of having a strong philosophical bent. This fact is seen in the display case in front of the church, which displays short, pithy samples of wisdom from the past. These sayings are changed frequently, and many Riversiders look forward to the next bits of philosophy to be displayed.

The small red sandstone church is a real gem set in the five blocks of historic buildings that stretch from Main Street to the railroad tracks on Mission Inn Avenue.

The Mansion Known as Rockledge

High above Ivy Street near Victoria Avenue stands an unforgettable mansion known as Rockledge. Its position high on a hillside provides it with a magnificent view of downtown Riverside below and to the northwest. Just how high is that mansion on the hill? I counted twenty-seven steps and three long, steep ramps to the house from Ivy Street. Jacqueline Hopper, who was kind enough to invite me for a visit, suggested that I drive up the driveway to the rear of the home. Instead, I made the climb from the street because I was so impressed with the home's height above the street and with its breathtaking view that extends to Mount Rubidoux and beyond.

Rockledge was built in 1889 by a young man named Priestley Hall, whose parents were both medical doctors. The physicians soon tired of the medical practice and went into the horticultural business, with real estate as a sideline. In those days, Riverside real estate often sold in plots of up to 180 acres.

Young Priestley Hall acquired large acreage holdings in the southwest part of Riverside, some of which came to be known as Hall's Additions. He chose some twenty acres of land overlooking Tequesquite Arroyo for his own home. Young Hall chose well, because that area is still choice real estate almost 125 years later.

The residence Hall built was a three-story home consisting of 4,500 square feet. Today, the home is on a parcel of one and a half acres. The foundation and walls of the large home were built from adobe brick, and the adobe is still in the house. In addition to the main house, there is a small carriage house with a garage below and a studio apartment above.

In a most romantic gesture, Priestley Hall married a young woman named Agnes Overton and gave her the deed to the home, now known as Rockledge, as a wedding present. Agnes was a singer who often sang as a soloist at Riverside weddings. The couple lived alone in the large home for twenty years. Hall was a nurseryman, and he added greenhouses and rare and decorative plants to the property. He brought in Franz Hosp, a landscape architect, to beautify the property. Hall even had peacocks that added beauty and noise to the neighborhood.

The land passed through several owners, and in 1942, the home was severely damaged by fire. A partial reconstruction followed. One set of owners was Wilton and Mildred Gerhardt. Wilton had traveled the world as an engineer for Bechtel Corporation. This couple made extensive alterations to the property, enhancing the Victorian appearance of the home.

The Gerhardts, in a grand gesture, offered to donate the Rockledge estate to the City of Riverside for use as the official mayor's residence. The city council, in its wisdom, felt that there were too many conditions to the grant, so the city declined the offer. Looking at the magnificent property that is Rockledge today, one can't help but question the judgment of the city council in turning down the gift of this choice property.

The Gerhardts deeded the property to the University of Redlands, and the university, in turn, sold the mansion and its grounds to Dr. Andrew Hopper and his wife, Jacqueline, in 1995. The Hoppers are the present owners of Rockledge.

This stunning residence's grounds have been open to the public in recent years as part of a garden tour sponsored by the Art Alliance of the Riverside Art Museum.

The Duchess of Corona

Mrs. Janet Gould was called "the Duchess" because of her regal bearing and her many contributions to her city and her state. Photos exist showing Mrs. Gould in the attire of a well-dressed woman of the early nineteenth century. She wore this outfit when she spoke to different organizations, as she often did. Her black dress was marked by a delicate pattern. She wore the mantilla in her hair that supported a black lace scarf. Her arms carried golden bracelets that jangled when she gestured during her talks.

She was born Janet Williams on a plantation in Howard County, Missouri, in 1878. Her father was a banker who served a term as treasurer of the state of Missouri. Early in life, Janet became interested in history, and it became a lifelong interest for her. She majored in history and English before marrying Walter M. Dean, who died in 1935. She married a second time to Chester Gould, who died in 1952.

Twice a widow and living in Corona, she became fascinated with the Indian artifacts found in the area around Corona and in the local Spanish and Mexican heritage. Mrs. Gould did research in such libraries as the Huntington Library in San Marino and the Bancroft Library in Berkeley. She wrote articles and poems, and she shared her accumulated knowledge by giving talks to clubs and church groups.

The "Duchess" title came to her, though no one knows who originated it. People in Corona generally accepted the title, though unofficial, as appropriate to this energetic and dignified lady. Mrs. Gould was most famous for her work in researching and publicizing the history of Corona. For the fiftieth anniversary of the city in 1936, Janet wrote and directed a pageant that was staged by schoolchildren. The city enjoyed the pageant, and people in Corona talked about it for years after the event.

Mrs. Gould used her influence to secure the establishment of state historical markers in and around Corona. One of them marks the site of the old Butterfield Stage Station on the old Corona-Elsinore Road.

The Duchess died in July 1964 at age eighty-six. She had lived in Corona for fifty-four years. She was recognized as the historical authority on Corona and its environs. She was often contacted by government officials for information relating to local history. Many of her papers and artifacts were donated to the Corona Public Library.

She left a son, a daughter, a stepdaughter and five grandchildren, as well as five great-grandchildren. Corona's Duchess made more of a contribution to her city and state than many of the officially titled duchesses of Europe make to their lands.

Part II
Early Twentieth Century

Riverside's 1908 Elephant Stampede

There's an old, very cynical joke about insurance companies. It holds that if insurers had their way, they would provide everyone with insurance against elephant stampedes. Such stampedes rarely occur, and rarer still are there resulting injuries. Therefore, insurance companies would have lots of money coming in and very little going out in the form of claims.

In April 1908, Riverside did have an elephant stampede, and with fatal results. The Sells-Floto Circus came to town and set up tents on Blaine Street (now Third Street) near Kansas Avenue, the same lot where I attended the circus as a kid in the mid-1940s.

It was a windy day that April 16, and a fire started at the nearby Standard Oil Company distribution center that resulted in the death of one Standard employee. That death would not be the last death in Riverside that day. Fiery ash and embers from the Standard fire hit the canvas tents of the Sells-Floto Circus. Four elephants, normally docile, panicked at the sight and smell of the fire. The elephants took off in all directions but mostly toward the center of downtown Riverside.

One of the crazed elephants, a male named Floto, chased a woman named Ella Gibbs, a Congregationalist and social worker. She tried to enter a house but was unable to gain entry. Floto charged onto the porch, knocked her down and trampled her to death. This took place at the southeast corner

Elephants from the Sells-Floto Circus are seen in downtown Riverside. *Courtesy of Riverside Metropolitan Museum.*

The fire at Standard Oil Company's Riverside distribution facility sparked the elephant stampede. *Courtesy of Riverside Metropolitan Museum.*

The elephants were soon rounded up. *Courtesy of Riverside Metropolitan Museum.*

of Fourth and Mulberry Streets, and the house still stands as of this writing. It now bears a fresh coat of blue and gray paint.

Alarmed citizens heard the commotion and ran into the streets, some firing shots at the rampaging beast, but to no avail. Floto continued his charge into downtown. At Seventh (now Mission Inn Avenue) and Orange Street, the elephant knocked down a Mission Inn laundryman named Gin Ung, but the man survived with no more than a broken rib.

The pachyderm charged onto the Mission Inn patio and into the hotel's barbershop, wreaking havoc all the way. Its final bit of destruction took place in a livery stable on Main Street. There, handlers from the circus finally gained control over the frightened animal.

What of the other three animals that had broken free and run from the circus? They were all soon recaptured, including one that had stopped in an orange grove near the Gage Canal to eat the famous Riverside navel oranges.

Despite the tragic death of an innocent woman, the other injuries and the heavy damage and destruction, many took delight in retelling the story, and the saga seemed to grow with each narration. News accounts stated that all of the damage claims against the circus were settled for $17,000. Ella Gibbs's family only asked for funeral expenses.

Colonel Roosevelt Met Ex-Slave

Theodore Roosevelt became an accidental president in 1901, but he became more influential than many of those who had been elected to the office. He was reelected in 1904 overwhelmingly. By 1911, Colonel Roosevelt, as he was often called, was an ex-president who was still active and very popular with the public. He had returned from an African big-game hunt that captured the public's imagination.

Politically, Roosevelt was part of the progressive movement that sought to curb the excesses of big business and to improve the lives of common people through such measures as conservation of forests and passage of the Pure Food and Drug Act. Socially, Colonel Roosevelt was ahead of his time. As president, he had created a stir when he invited a black leader, Booker T. Washington, to lunch at the White House.

In 1911, Reverend R.W. Mottern of Riverside learned that a former slave living in Riverside had memories of the family, and fellow slaves, of Roosevelt's mother, whose maiden name was Martha Bullock. Martha supported the Confederate cause during the Civil War, and one of her brothers served as an admiral in the Confederate navy.

The former slave was named Moses Bacon, and by 1911, he was an elderly man whose mind was still alert and blessed with a good memory. Following receipt of a letter from Reverend Mottern, he and Moses Bacon were invited to meet the ex-president at the Hotel Maryland in Pasadena. In March, 1911, Reverend Mottern and Moses Bacon boarded the Salt Lake Railroad train from the railroad station that still stands on Vine Street near Mission Inn Avenue for the trip to Pasadena.

Former president Roosevelt and his secretary met the reverend and Moses Bacon in the lobby of the hotel. The meeting between the former president and the black man was novel enough that a crowded lobby witnessed the interview. Roosevelt shook the hands of both visitors and proceeded to ask Moses Bacon questions about life on the Georgia plantation where Bacon had served the Bullock family as a slave. Moses Bacon was able to answer correctly every question posed by Roosevelt. He was able to name his fellow household slaves. Bacon's answers matched the information Roosevelt had learned from his mother and from his aunts.

Roosevelt's secretary asked him to cut the interview short because of a dinner engagement in the hotel, but the former president refused to leave

President Theodore "Teddy" Roosevelt spoke to enthusiastic crowds at Riverside, toured the city and planted trees in an earlier visit. *Courtesy of Riverside Metropolitan Museum.*

until he had discussed fully the family situation that had existed in Cobb County, Georgia, in those days before the Civil War.

When the Roosevelt entourage finally departed for the dinner engagement, a reporter from the *Los Angeles Express* continued to ask questions of Moses Bacon and Reverend R.W. Mottern, who had made the trip to Pasadena from Riverside. This anecdote illustrates the sympathy Roosevelt had for ex-slaves and the interest he had in his mother's family background on a plantation in Georgia almost fifty years before the meeting held in a Pasadena hotel.

ARSENIC IN THE PANCAKES

In November 1917, the nation was involved in what was then called the Great War (later termed World War I). Citizens were encouraged to buy war bonds and to "Hooverize," which meant to reduce consumption of meat and wheat so that American troops and Allied forces would have enough food.

In Arlington, the family of forty-year-old Albert J. Schneider, a local jeweler, sat down to eat a light lunch of pancakes (no meat). All three who ate the pancakes became violently ill and died within a few hours. Medical examiners found arsenic poisoning as the cause of the three deaths. At first, investigators thought that the poison had been contained in the silver polish found in the home at 675 Miller Street. Later searches found a container of arsenic on the porch of the home some distance from the kitchen.

Arsenic was at first thought to have been placed in the pancakes by error. The grandmother, one of the three victims, was an eighty-year-old woman whose eyesight was not good. Officials thought that she had used the arsenic powder instead of baking powder in her pancake batter. The fact that arsenic was found in both the pancakes and in the fruit syrup that was used by the family for the midday meal cast doubt on that theory and suggested intentional poisoning. Nonetheless, the official finding of the inquest was that the deaths of all three in the Schneider family were caused by an accidental substitution of arsenic for baking powder in the pancake batter.

Murder by poison is often described in the mystery novels of Agatha Christie and other British writers, but more than one observer has noted that Americans seldom poison their victims; they are far more likely to shoot them. At the very least, the Schneider case leaves several unanswered questions. How could the aged grandmother make a mistake and substitute arsenic for baking powder when the arsenic container was on the porch and far from the kitchen cupboard? Was the amount of arsenic sufficient to kill three people greater than the usual amount of baking powder used in pancake batter? From the sudden deaths of all three persons, young and old, one might suspect that this was true. Was there a person who had a motive to kill the Schneiders? Was there a visitor to the home in hours or days before the deaths who had access to the arsenic on the porch?

We will never know the answers to these and other questions surrounding the mysterious deaths by poisoning in November 1917. We are left with the haunting suspicion that someone, person or persons unknown, died with knowledge of the poisoning of the Schneider family that was not disclosed to the investigators of the time. Was it a terrible accident, or was it murder? After more than ninety years, we will never know for certain.

Stores in Arlington were closed for the time of the Schneider family funeral as a gesture of community respect.

CHARLIE HITCHENS PAID A HEAVY PRICE

Some old soldiers generalize and say that, in war, there are those who lead and those who follow. The leaders win the glory, and the followers win the war. True or not, there are those who pay a heavier price in war than others. One who paid a terrible price was Charlie Hitchens, an ordinary infantryman in World War I, a war that began almost a century ago. I don't know whether Charlie rose to become sergeant or not. Probably he did not. He was an ordinary soldier in the trenches.

Charlie grew up in Steamboat Springs, Colorado. When the United States entered World War I in April 1917, to make the world safe for democracy, Charlie was one of the first to volunteer. He was strong and healthy. He had grown up breathing the clear air of the Rocky Mountains, an irony considering what was to befall Charlie.

Off in France, under the overall command of General John J. "Black Jack" Pershing, American soldiers were at first merged with French and British units. But Pershing was determined to keep his U.S. Army units separate from those of the tired and often dejected units of the European Allies.

In early combat, the U.S. Army and Marine Corps distinguished themselves in such battles as the Argonne, Belleau Wood and Chateau Thierry. The German generals could see that the fresh, eager American divisions would soon overwhelm their tired, dispirited troops. By the time the American troops arrived, both German and Allied forces were using poison gases of various types—mustard gas, chlorine gas and other deadly concoctions. These gas shells were so deadly and potent that when dug up ninety years later, they still exuded a lethal gas.

The Allies tried several defenses against poison gas, starting with an almost futile wet rag hung across the nose and mouth. Later, gas masks were issued to the troops. Charlie Hitchens was gassed, and his lungs were severely damaged. In the army of the day, a macho spirit prevailed; he was treated and sent back to his unit, still wheezing and coughing.

The war ended in November 1918, and Charlie's unit was chosen for occupation duty. U.S. forces occupied a portion of western Germany. Charlie later told friends that the defeated German civilians were friendlier to Americans than were the French. Such are the ironies of war.

Charlie returned home to Steamboat Springs, still wheezing and gasping for breath. He married his high school sweetheart, Leota, and worked in a variety of fields. Carpentry and cabinetmaking were his specialties. Charlie and Leota had one son.

The Hitchens family moved to California in search of a healthier environment for Charlie's crippled lungs. They settled in Rosemead and later moved to Riverside, where they bought a home on Ottawa Avenue near Patterson Park. Knowing Charlie's health-destroying experience in the war, one might expect the Hitchens to discourage their son from entering military service. Just the opposite took place. Floyd Hitchens joined the U.S. Air Force and became a pilot.

I knew Charlie and Leota Hitchens as neighbors forty years after World War I, and it was sad to see Charlie gasping for every breath. It seems he could walk for only a few steps before needing to stop to regain his breath.

In January 1962, Charlie died. Some would say that death was a blessing for this incurably wounded man whose every breath was a torment. Charlie's son asked me to be a pallbearer at Charlie's funeral. I was honored to accept. The old soldier had suffered greatly in the army and for the rest of his life. One could argue that his many years of painful breathing constituted a greater suffering than that of the men who were shot and killed on the field of battle.

In 1962, the military cemetery near the March air base had not yet been built. Charlie was laid to rest at the Rose Hills Cemetery near Whittier. His widow, Leota, lived on for a few years before she, too, passed away.

Fast-forward fifty years from Charlie's war to the Vietnam War, in which the U.S. military used 19 million gallons of the toxic herbicide Agent Orange. The idea was to kill jungle foliage where the enemy hid. Agent Orange killed the foliage, and it also delivered injuries to U.S. troops. Some of these injuries, such as leukemia, would not appear until years after exposure to the chemical. The U.S. Department of Veterans Affairs indicates that 100,000 troops were exposed to Agent Orange.

Common sense would suggest that any chemical capable of turning a jungle brown within hours would not be good for human contact. As in Charlie's war, there was the inevitable blowback. Unpredictable winds would blow the gas or herbicide back into the faces of the troops who had launched the chemical or who happened to be in the area.

The Jerry Pettis Veterans' Hospital was able to tell me the number of veterans being treated for diabetes, but not the number being treated for Agent Orange injuries. I have interviewed two of the affected men. One man, confined to a wheelchair, showed me sores on his immobile legs, injuries due to Agent Orange exposure. Another veteran, a retired officer, has lost feeling in his fingertips (neuropathy), which his doctor attributes to Agent Orange. Press reports during the past two or three years indicate that veterans' hospitals have not been caring properly for severely injured veterans of recent wars, wars that continue halfway around the world.

Each Memorial Day, if the honored fallen warriors like Charlie Hitchens could speak again, I believe that they would tell us that it is more important to care for the injured servicemen who live among us than to honor the dead from past wars.

Armistice Celebrated in Arlington

World War I ended in November 1918, brought about by an armistice, and that meant an end to fighting but not a final peace settlement. Still, it was a time of joy and celebration across the land and, closer to home, in Arlington, a section of Riverside. Many years later, Armistice Day became Veterans Day.

When the news of the armistice was announced near midnight, Pacific Time, in long ago 1918, bells rang, shots were fired into the sky and every type of noise filled the air. A bonfire was lit in the center of the intersection at Magnolia and Van Buren Avenues. Manager J.H. Jennings of the Lewis grocery store grabbed a box of cigars from his stock and began passing them out to men on the street. The noise and the bonfire continued all night. Before dawn, someone strung up from a lamppost a dummy labeled "Kaiser Bill." The intended subject of the effigy was Kaiser Wilhelm II of Germany.

There was a well-respected cannery in Arlington at that time. It canned tomatoes, sweet potatoes and fruit such as apricots, depending on the season. Employed at the Arlington Cannery were a few men who had immigrated to the United States from Italy. Italy was one of the victorious Allied nations in 1918, and a group of these Italian-born cannery workers grabbed a company truck and covered it with an Italian flag. This truck, filled with joyful, singing Italians, made its way through the crowded streets of Arlington.

Many of the people celebrating the victory decided that they would drive to Riverside, where the larger city promised to have a larger celebration. Trucks and cars were piled with people, and the vehicles drove toward Riverside with horns sounding and occupants singing. Celebrations continued in Riverside as people celebrated the end of the "war to end all wars," as Allied propaganda had promised.

The Armistice Day Parade in Arlington memorializes the end of the "war to end all wars." *Courtesy of Riverside Metropolitan Museum.*

This modern shot of the corner of Van Buren and Magnolia Avenues depicts the Jensen Building that was in use during the armistice celebration of 1918. *Photo by the author.*

The people of Southern California were convinced that all of their sacrifices had been worthwhile and that only peace, prosperity and a bright future awaited them. The *Arlington Times* carried a front-page article stating that the Arlington Cannery would increase the size of its plant. There was talk of the California legislature establishing a facility near Arlington that would provide dozens of jobs.

Locally, nationally and internationally, November 1918 was a time of great hope for the future. The period of readjustment was a painful one, and news of the Versailles Treaty seemed to carry with it a harsh peace that would embitter Germany. The U.S. Senate rejected the Versailles Treaty, and there were indications that both Europe and Asia would soon spew forth new aggression and warfare. Little more than twenty years after that ecstatic celebration of the 1918 armistice, Europe was at war again. Asia had been at war since 1931, when Japan invaded China's province of Manchuria.

Of the people who celebrated so enthusiastically that November in 1918, many of them were able to live long enough to see the United States swept into war once again in December 1941. The Allies had won the war that ended in 1918 but somehow had managed to lose the peace that followed, and a second world war more terrible than the first came to bedevil mankind.

HEROINE OF THE 1918 INFLUENZA BATTLE

Riverside produced a heroine and selfless martyr who has not been given enough recognition. This person was a student nurse named Charlotte Waggoner Fay, who graduated in 1916 from Riverside Girls High School. She was called to help with the overload at Riverside City Hospital during the influenza pandemic of 1918.

Charlotte worked around the clock to assist many of the victims of the terrible flu. Not yet a registered nurse, she gave the profession her all. Often the sufferers of influenza would appear to recover, only to die from a secondary infection, such as pneumonia or tuberculosis.

Unwilling to leave the sick persons in her charge, Charlotte worked to the point of exhaustion. In this weakened state, she caught the flu and died on October 28, 1918. World War I was still raging, and Charlotte was not yet twenty-two years old. She had worked in the nursing field for two years.

Charlotte W. Fay was a brave nurse who worked around the clock, caring for the sick and dying during the influenza outbreak of 1918. The local post of the Disabled American Veterans is named for her. *Photo by the author.*

At her funeral, Riverside mourned the passing of this beautiful, selfless nurse who had given of herself to assist those who were suffering. Some of those she nursed were soldiers from the Alessandro Flight School. At her graveside service, a flight of aircraft from the future March Field flew over the Evergreen Cemetery and dropped flowers onto the assembled mourners. This was a rare tribute by the military to a civilian. In the eyes of Riversiders of the time, Charlotte Fay was a selfless heroine who was at least the equal of Florence Nightingale, the English founder of the modern nursing profession.

Frank Miller and the Spanish Writer

Vicente Blasco-Ibanez was an important Spanish writer who visited the Mission Inn in 1920. His visit isn't mentioned in most books about the Mission Inn and its important visitors, and for good reason: the Spaniard spent little more than one hour in the inn during his visit. It is notable that the visitor from Spain admired the inn and its many works of Spanish art. He vowed to make a return visit to Riverside and the Mission Inn, although that's not recorded.

During Blasco-Ibanez's visit to the inn, he had lunch in the dining room. Frank Miller, proprietor of the Mission Inn, was always eager to welcome and honor visiting dignitaries in his hotel. During the meal, Miller had his three-piece orchestra, specially assembled for the occasion, play the Spanish

Frank Miller, the master of the Mission Inn, was one of Riverside's most prominent citizens and host to presidents and Hollywood royalty. *Courtesy of Riverside Metropolitan Museum.*

national hymn or anthem. Miller believed that Blasco-Ibanez would be pleased to hear the national anthem of his native Spain. Instead, he was annoyed. He credited Miller with good intentions, but the national hymn of Spain was associated with the monarchy of King Alfonso XIII, and Blasco-Ibanez was an ardent republican opposed to all monarchies, especially that of his homeland. This occasion was one of the few times that Miller's attempt to honor a very important person went awry.

The Spanish writer claimed that the inn reminded him of churches in his native Spain, particularly those of his birthplace, Valencia. The works of Blasco-Ibanez were popular around the world, and Hollywood produced four movie versions of his novels. The first of the Spaniard's books to be filmed was *The Four Horsemen of the Apocalypse*. The 1921 silent film of this novel made Rudolph Valentino a star. The story of loyalty and tragedy in the First World War was so powerful that it won public acclaim.

Probably the best known of his works to be adapted by Hollywood was *Blood and Sand*, the 1941 film that vaulted Rita Hayworth to stardom. It also stars Tyrone Power. This film centers on bullfighting, and its closing line is unforgettable. A character states that the only beast in the bullfighting arena is the crowd.

Young Hero Saved a Life While Losing His Own

The word "hero" is overused, but this story describes the actions of a twelve-year-old boy who would qualify as hero by almost anyone's definition.

In the summer of 1923, a group of young Rialto residents drove to the Mockingbird Lake south of Riverside to picnic and to fish. The group consisted of Elizabeth Roberts, her husband and their baby, Jim, plus Elizabeth's sister, Mary, and several friends. The group enjoyed the beautiful day at the lake. They sang songs and ate their basket lunch. As the group was about to drive home, Mary, age thirteen, approached the irrigation ditch to get the baby a drink of water. Suddenly, an automatic gate was raised, and water roared in, sweeping Mary into the lake. Mary's sister, Elizabeth, age seventeen, tried to rescue her sister while holding the baby. Both mother and child were swept into the fast-moving water. Neither of the young women knew how to swim.

Nearby, there was an unrelated twelve-year-old boy who saw the emergency and jumped into the water. He brought the infant out safely. He jumped into the lake again in an effort to save the two sisters, but in the panic and confusion, the girls pulled the boy into the water. The two sisters and the boy, Ron Huber of Riverside, all drowned that afternoon. Ron Huber was an orphan whose father had died in World War I. He was being raised by his grandmother.

The loss of the two young women shocked the community of Rialto, a town so small that everyone seemed to know one another in 1923. The selfless and heroic action of the Riverside youth was also acclaimed. The rescued baby, Jim Burton, was raised by his father. He grew to be a healthy adult, and he remembered nothing of that terrible day when he was rescued and his mother and aunt drowned. Burton served in the army in World War II and returned to Rialto, where he had a career as a letter carrier. He lives today, approaching age ninety, in the family home in Rialto.

Jim Burton had children, grandchildren and great-grandchildren, all of whom never would have been born had he not been saved by the valiant, self-sacrificing boy from Riverside, Ron Huber. True heroes are few, and most of us will never have the opportunity to perform a truly heroic deed. The definition of hero I prefer is taken from my dictionary: one who is "supremely noble or self-sacrificing." Almost ninety years ago, a Riverside boy matched or exceeded that definition. I can find no evidence that Ron Huber was awarded a medal for his heroism. Surely, if any civilian deserved a medal for heroism, it was Ron Huber.

Neighbors of Woodcraft Retirement Home

The Women of Woodcraft began as an auxiliary to the Woodmen of the World Lodge in the 1890s. Twenty years later, the Women of Woodcraft changed their name to Neighbors of Woodcraft. This organization was a benefit society in which members provided for one another in case of serious illness or death of the breadwinner.

For more than thirty years, there was a retirement home for the Neighbors of Woodcraft on Magnolia Avenue between Adams Street and Monroe Street. Many of the buildings from the retirement home still exist. They form the older part, the northern part, of the California Baptist University.

The Neighbors' home consisted of rooms for the retirees and some of the staff. The home had a library, a large dining room and a lobby for visitors. It had a laundry that operated around the clock. The home originally sat on a parcel of land slightly larger than seventy-five acres.

In an article that appeared in the *Arlington Times* in July 1945, Mrs. Minnie Hiner was profiled. She held the title of "Grand Guardian" of the Neighbors of Woodcraft, with headquarters in Portland, Oregon. Several retirees were interviewed for the article, and all were enthusiastic about living in the Neighbors' retirement home. Motorists driving by on Magnolia Avenue, morning or afternoon, could see the residents seated in chairs watching the traffic go by as they discussed their careers and their grandchildren.

There was a Riverside group of the Neighbors of Woodcraft called the Ragged Robin Circle. This group met several times each month to socialize and discuss lodge business. Members of any one of the circles for fifteen years or more who had reached the age of sixty-five were eligible to retire in the Riverside retirement home. That home was an almost self-sufficient manor, with a large farm on the home's extensive acreage. The farm manager raised beef cattle and had more than one thousand chickens. A variety of crops was raised to provide the residents with fresh fruit and vegetables. The retirement home even had a small hospital for those residents too ill or infirm to live in one of the rooms. The home had its own physician and nurses on staff.

In 1954, the governing board of California Baptist College purchased the land and buildings from the Neighbors of Woodcraft whose retirees had declined in number. Cal Baptist has maintained many of the Neighbors' old buildings and has added modern buildings to the south and east of the old structures.

Gone is the Neighbors' old farm, the land being turned into playing fields and parking lots. Replacing the retirement home is a large, modern university with 4,700 students.

Wild and Exotic Animals in Fairmount Park

The public expects such wild animals as raccoons, skunks and 'possums to find their way into Fairmount Park, once Riverside's largest park. Some eighty or ninety years ago, though, even more exotic animals resided in the park, and Riverside even had a zoo for two or three years.

In the 1920s, there was an ostrich named Queen that was kept in an enclosure in Fairmount Park. People fed it, as might be expected, but upon the bird's death, it was found that the ostrich's stomach contained forty-nine pennies and other assorted small metal objects. Visitors to the park were throwing these nonfood items to the bird, knowing that the creature was not a very discriminating eater.

In 1933, Riverside established a zoo on the northern shore of Fairmount Lake, right across from the boathouse. Architect Henry Jekel was one of the moving forces behind the zoo. Used lumber from the old fairgrounds was used to build a structure to house native and exotic animals.

A female lion was one of the most popular animals of the zoo. The Seventy-ninth Pursuit Squadron of March Field found and captured a cinnamon bear during one of its firefighting missions. The bear was given a home in the zoo. Other animals included a bald eagle, a raven, a badger and two monkeys. The monkeys were named Maggie and Jiggs after popular cartoon characters of the day. Riversider Bob Tabor worked up a show starring the two monkeys. Schoolchildren and their teachers were often invited to see both the show and the animals for free. Others had to pay a ten-cent admission charge to the zoo.

By 1935, some of the animals had died, and the public lost interest in the zoo. The city was reluctant to continue funding the zoo, and it was closed. The buildings stood until the late 1940s, when they found their final use as part of Poly High teacher and coach Bob Hallock's day camp for children. Later, a small amusement park was built on the former zoo site by Ray Watson and Leo Barnes. The park included a carousel, a miniature train that ran on a circular track and one or two other rides. Next to the amusement park there was a miniature golf course. Today, all of the amusement activities mentioned have been removed.

In the late 1950s, there was an effort to set up a small children's petting zoo, but this effort was unsuccessful. Parents desiring to take their children to a zoo today have two choices. They may visit the Los Angeles Zoo or, by driving farther, visit the much larger San Diego Zoo.

Stars Flocked to the Norconian

The Norconian Hotel and resort was one of those dream complexes built in the 1920s by wealthy people who were able to carry those dreams to reality. Among the builders of dream structures in that period were William Randolph Hearst, who built his castle at San Simeon in central California. Another was Ellen Browning Scripps, who built a women's college in Claremont. Yet a third builder was Rex Clark, who built the Norconian in Norco. Coincidentally, all three dream structures were paid for by fortunes from newspaper chains. Both Miss Scripps's fortune and that of Rex Clark came from the Scripps-Howard newspaper chain.

An examination of Scripps College in Claremont will suggest similarities with the Norconian Hotel. Both are built in the Spanish-Mediterranean Revival style, and both structures feature murals, sculpture and art throughout.

The Norconian in the late 1920s and 1930s attracted many stars of stage and screen. Comedians Buster Keaton, Stan Laurel and Joe E. Brown made films there. Mae West and Greta Garbo stayed there. Bob Hope and Robert Montgomery were often seen there.

In the world of sport, the Norconian's Olympic-size swimming pool was used as a training site for swimmers preparing for the 1928 and 1932 Olympic games. Johnny Weissmuller, who later starred as Tarzan in the movies, trained there. More than one world swimming record was set at the Norconian pool. Duke Kahanamoku demonstrated swim and surfing techniques at the resort's lake. Babe Ruth also enjoyed the Norconian on a brief visit.

Celebrities' visits increased at the Norconian after it became the Norco Naval Hospital in 1941. Actors and actresses visited the hospital to cheer up U.S. Navy and Marine Corps patients and to show that the nation, and the film colony, wished them well. First Lady Eleanor Roosevelt showed Washington's interest in the hospital and its patients as she dropped by to wish the servicemen a speedy recovery.

In 1948, my father, a U.S. Navy veteran of both world wars, was a patient in the hospital. He often spoke of the visit by actor George Raft to the hospital wards. My father had seen several of Raft's gangster films. A long list of stars visited the navy hospital: Cary Grant, Errol Flynn, Jack Benny, Humphrey Bogart, Gary Cooper, Claudette Colbert and Red Skelton.

Today, the formerly elegant Norconian is vacant and fenced. The roof has finally been covered to prevent further water damage. Kevin Bash, a Norco councilman, has called for federal and local funding to restore the historic and artistic treasure. Bash has written a book titled *The Norconian Resort*.

Amelia Earhart's Mission Inn Visit

Amelia Earhart, often called the "First Lady of Aviation," visited Riverside in 1928 and stayed at the Mission Inn. By 1936, she had become famous and was invited to place her wings on the Fliers Wall of the Mission Inn.

DeWitt V. Hutchings of the Mission Inn and Amelia Earhart are entertained by the hotel's resident parrots. *Courtesy of Riverside Metropolitan Museum.*

This wall is on the second floor near the entrance to the St. Francis Chapel, a popular wedding spot.

Earhart began her career in aviation in Los Angeles by paying $1,000 for a series of flight lessons taught by another woman, Neta Snook, who had learned to fly in the Curtiss Flying School. Snook was the first woman admitted to that school.

Earhart flew across the Atlantic Ocean as a passenger and was immediately called "Lady Lindbergh" because she was the first woman to make the transatlantic flight. In 1932, Earhart flew solo across the Atlantic, again the first woman to do so.

In August 1932, Earhart was honored by a military review and flyover at March Field. Records at the March Field Air Museum indicate that Earhart flew into Riverside at least three times. Earhart married George Putnam, a wealthy publisher, after rejecting his proposals four times. He was a strong supporter of her flying missions, and his wealth made them possible.

In June 1937, Earhart began an around-the-world trip by air in Miami that was to include Africa, New Guinea and the vast Pacific Ocean. She made it safely to Lae, New Guinea, in her Lockheed Electra twin-engine plane. She was accompanied by her navigator, Fred Noonan, a known alcoholic.

Heavily loaded with fuel, Earhart's aircraft took off from New Guinea, headed for Howland Island, a tiny uninhabited isle in the South Pacific. She never reached that island. Navy and Coast Guard planes and many ships were unable to find any trace of the two fliers or their aircraft. From time to time, there are reports of the discovery of what someone believes is Earhart's tennis shoe or a piece of the Lockheed Electra. There was even a report that she had ventured into Japanese-held islands and was beheaded as a spy.

Not one of these theories has been confirmed, and most have been discredited. The fate of Amelia Earhart and her navigator thus rates as one of the great mysteries of the twentieth century.

Riverside's Mission Inn still has the wings that Amelia Earhart nailed to the Fliers Wall, and the wings carry her hand-carved initials, "A.E." There are photos that show Amelia smiling as she was honored at the wall. Patricia Korzec, director of the March Field Air Museum, has performed a flying history program for school and civic groups in which she dresses as Earhart and pretends to be the famous flier. Those who have seen the program tell me that it's very good.

Startling Similarities, Eighty-two Years Apart

Does history repeat itself? Let us examine two very similar cases that took place almost eighty-two years apart and involved two men who served as chief of Riverside's police department. John Franklin was chief of police in Riverside, a city of thirty thousand people in 1928. He was a close friend of Mayor E.M. Dighton.

In early May 1928, Chief Franklin was arrested for public drunkenness on a side street in Colton with a friend named W.C. Smith. Being drunk in public was an especially serious offense in 1928 because prohibition was the law of the land. Of course, most people also felt that the chief of police should uphold and enforce the law, not break the law. The Colton chief of police gave his fellow police chief from across the county line no leniency. Riverside's Chief Franklin spent several hours in the Colton jail that early May morning. The next day, Riverside's Mayor Dighton suspended his friend the police chief.

Fast-forward almost eighty-two years to a night in mid-February 2010 with a different police chief and a much larger Riverside. Riverside in early 2010 had a population of about 300,000 people and was a far different place from the Riverside of 1928.

Russ Leach, the police chief of 2010, apparently had a few drinks in a bar in Colton. Allegedly, Chief Leach drove erratically and crashed his city-owned vehicle into a fireplug and a pole before driving on for three miles. Though the 2010 incident may be viewed as more serious than that of 1928, Riverside police officers apparently were more lenient to the disoriented driver before them. Possibly the leniency of 2010 was due to the fact that the officers were dealing with their boss.

In 1928, the drunken Riverside police chief was given no slack by the Colton police chief. The 2010 incident did result in the prompt resignation of Riverside's chief. The mayor did not have an opportunity to suspend his twenty-first-century chief.

There are remarkable coincidences in the two incidents involving actual or alleged public drunkenness by men who, at different times, served as chief of police of Riverside. Both cases involved the automobile, though the chief of 1928 was merely sitting and drinking in his car, while the chief of 2010 went on a wild, destructive ride in his city-owned vehicle. Finally, there is the city of Colton, watering hole of choice for Riverside police chiefs even after eighty-two years.

While the similarities between the two incidents may be striking, it is fair to state that history *never* repeats itself in exactly the same way. The times are different, of course, and the individuals involved are usually different, as well as timing and the location of events. One last point on the 1928 event: Chief Franklin's friend, Mayor E.M. Dighton, was probably harmed politically by Franklin's arrest. Dighton was recalled a few months later, and to this day he is the only mayor of Riverside to be recalled and removed from office.

Honeyed Words of Bad Times

Depression and recession—I call them bad times. These bad times bring forth ingenious promises and claims in order to move products and sell tickets. In 1930, there was a custom, now almost forgotten, that the downtown Fox Riverside theater would have a Wednesday housewives movie matinee.

Housewives would be invited to a special movie at a reduced price. Many women made it their Wednesday afternoon habit.

One of the popular films of 1930 was *Honey*, a comedy that starred ZaSu Pitts. Due to the Depression, attendance was down at the Wednesday matinee. In order to increase attendance at the showing of *Honey*, the Fox management promised a jar of honey to each woman who attended the housewives matinee. Incidentally, Riverside County at the time was one of the top producers of honey in California.

The story about honey is only one example of how bad times seem to bring forth ingenious, even desperate, advertising appeals. As this is being written, apartment houses, storefronts and warehouses often show signs that read "Now Renting," "For Lease" or simply "Available." Retailers often voice their desperation with such appeals as "40% off."

In the mid-1930s, several owners of Riverside downtown restaurants banded together to sponsor a newspaper advertisement that read, "Take her out to dinner once each week."

Much more hard-hitting was the mid-1930s advertisement that depicted an unattractive woman shown above the caption, "I don't shop at stores in Riverside. They ain't got no style." This negative advertisement concluded with the words, "Don't be a SCOOT," which was defined in the advertisement as a person who "Spends Cash Out of Town." The ad ended with the appeal, "Dollars spent at home come back to the spender. Keep your money in Riverside County."

Conditions may be bad today, but they were far worse in the mid-1930s before today's safety net was put in place. That safety net consists of unemployment insurance, food stamps and welfare payments. Some hungry people were so desperate that they walked in front of moving cars in order to receive hoped-for payment from the car owner's insurance company. At least they would be warm and well fed in the hospital, they figured.

Even professors of economics have a tough time making sense of today's conditions. Are we in recovery or will the recession continue for many months? Some even speak of a possible double-dip recession. While we are well off compared to some European countries such as Spain, which has more than 20 percent unemployed, some reports indicate that the two-county inland area has a 14 percent unemployment rate.

My favorite commercial appeal came from a sign recently placed in front of a carpet shop on Indiana Avenue. It read, "Cheap, Cheap Prices."

COLONEL HAP ARNOLD IN RIVERSIDE

Henry Harley "Hap" Arnold was the only U.S. Air Force officer to hold five-star rank, and he learned to fly under the personal instruction of the Wright brothers. He was the second pilot to be rated in the history of the U.S. military services.

Arnold was born in Gladwyne, Pennsylvania, and originally he planned to become a Baptist minister. He took the West Point test largely to please his father. As a cadet at the military academy, he earned demerits for pranks. He also played football, hurled the shot and rode a horse to play polo. He graduated in the bottom half of his class and was commissioned in the infantry in 1907. He was sent to the Philippine Islands, where he volunteered for the Signal Corps' mapping unit. Contacts made there aided him in joining the Aeronautical Division of the Signal Corps.

Arnold became a friend of Lieutenant George C. Marshall and Major Billy Mitchell, both rising stars in the U.S. Army. He joined Mitchell in advocating a separate U.S. Air Force. During World War I, Arnold held several administrative positions and became the youngest full colonel in the army. He developed influenza and spent the last few months of the war in an army hospital. With the end of the war and the reduction of personnel, Arnold was reduced in rank from colonel to his permanent rank of captain. The road to high rank had its setbacks.

Arnold could have had a profitable career in civilian life. He was offered the position of president of the newly formed Pan American World Airways but preferred to stay in the army. In his spare time, he wrote six books of fiction designed for young people. He was married and had several children.

Rising in rank again, Lieutenant Colonel Arnold became commanding officer of March Field near Riverside in 1931. He rebuilt the base and improved relations with the leading citizens of Riverside by requiring his officers to join a Riverside service club such as Rotary or Kiwanis. His planes made food drops to isolated communities during the bitter winter of 1932–33. He helped organize camps for the New Deal's Civilian Conservation Corps (CCC), and he hosted Hollywood stars who visited March Field, a base Arnold had made into a military showplace.

After General Westover was killed in an air crash in 1938, President Franklin Roosevelt named Arnold to head the U.S. Army Air Corps, with the rank of major general. This appointment was made despite Arnold's opponents charging that he was an alcoholic. Arnold was far-seeing, and he encouraged the development of the B-17 Flying Fortress bomber. He insisted on the production of a jet engine as soon as he learned of the invention from the British.

Right after the Japanese attack on Pearl Harbor, Arnold was made lieutenant general. He decided to use the limited number of B-29 Superfortress bombers only in the Pacific Theater, and he demanded more fighter escort for his bombers over Germany.

The war ended in 1945 with Arnold holding five-star rank. Some lower-ranking personnel believe that generals have an easy time of it. Arnold suffered from ulcers and had five heart attacks during the lead up to and fighting in World War II. He lost three fingers in one of his three plane crashes.

General Hap Arnold is still remembered fondly in Riverside. The Officers' Club at the March air base was named for him. Arnold Heights was a housing tract built for military families nearby. One Riverside woman, Nickie Shannon, a Poly High graduate in the class of 1951, recalls that Colonel Arnold bounced her on his knee when she was an infant and he was commanding officer of March Field. Mrs. Shannon's father was one of the flying officers stationed at the base.

General Arnold died in 1950 at age sixty-three.

Jurupa Harvest Festival Makes Comeback

In the darkest days of the Great Depression, in 1932, the people of the Jurupa Valley established the first of many harvest festivals. As one of the founders explained, conditions were so bad that "[w]e had to do something."

The Jurupa area was divided into five parts for purposes of competition: Glen Avon, West Riverside (today's Rubidoux), Mira Loma, Jurupa (today's Pedley) and Crestmore. Races were held, baseball games were played and awards were given for best exhibits. In one of the attractions, a boy of fifteen demonstrated his strength by getting on all fours and head-butting a goat as the crowd laughed and cheered.

The first festivals were held at the old West Riverside School. The sponsors could not afford a tent, so exhibits were crowded into the school's corridors. The most profitable of the shows in that first year was the cat display. People paid to see a woman's housecats.

Roman Warren and Tom Clay were two of the well-known citizens of the Jurupa Valley who acted in the *Trail of De Anza* pageant. This program was written by C.C. Bell of Glen Avon and was performed, in costume, at several of the early festivals. Jesse Wright even wrote a special song, "West Riverside," for the harvest festival.

Socially, the two-day event of 1932 was a great success. Economically, it was much less notable. After expenses were met, the festival netted only $18.74. The cat booth brought in $4.19 as the top money-earner.

By 1939, the festival had its own grounds at the location of the present Jurupa Cultural Center on Granite Hill Drive. The festival became an annual event until World War II, and then there were several years of a break. The festival resumed at the end of the war for several years. Meanwhile, sponsors of the festival were entering exhibits in the National Orange Show and the Pomona County Fair. Their exhibits won a surprising number of awards, bringing notice to the Jurupa Valley.

The festival association donated land to the California Department of Forestry, which built that attractive stone building that still stands on Mission Boulevard. The State of California took some of the association's land for construction of the 60 Freeway. The remaining eighty-four acres holds the Jurupa Cultural Center, which operates today as a museum and much more. Its metal mammoth looks down on Highway 60 from a hill on the center's property.

For the resumption of this festival, I can't help wondering if a brave youth can be found who will revive the practice of head-butting a goat.

LOCAL BROTHERS INTERVIEWED HITLER

The year was 1932, a few months before Adolf Hitler assumed power as chancellor of Germany. Two brothers from Riverside County managed to interview Hitler in his Munich headquarters of the Nazi Party. Herbert C. Schultz, a jeweler from Riverside, and his brother, Henry C. Schultz of Elsinore, were traveling in Germany with their German cousin as guide. The cousin was a prominent member of the Nazi Party, and he was able to arrange the meeting with Hitler.

With the German cousin acting as interpreter, the three men met Hitler in a large but spare office. Brownshirted Nazis guarded the leader carefully.

Hitler was pleased to meet with the Schultz brothers because they were of German descent and they belonged to German groups in California. Hitler explained that under his leadership Germany would pay no reparations to France or Belgium for damage caused by German invasion in World War I. One of the brothers asked what his response would be if France invaded Germany. Hitler replied firmly that France would not do that because Germany would repel any attacks with new, modern weapons.

When asked about Nazi policy toward Jews, Hitler answered that he would remove them from positions of influence such as newspaper editors. He also promised full compensation for property seized from Jewish owners. He gave no hint of the persecutions and mass murders that were to come later under the Hitler regime.

Hitler attacked the Communists for their lack of patriotism. He downplayed the dictatorship aspects that both Nazis and Communists shared. Hitler gave his version of German history to the three visitors, who sat in rapt attention. He told of the First Empire (or Reich), a union of small states. The Second Empire came after the Franco-Prussian War, lasting from 1870 until German defeat in 1918. The Third Empire would come under Nazi Party leadership, he promised.

The two Schultz brothers noted that Hitler was, for the most part, calm during the interview, though once he rose from his desk to wave his arms in the air to emphasize one of the points he made. The Führer was interested enough in his American visitors to grant them extended time for the interview. The brothers and their cousin left Hitler's office feeling honored that they had been received by the rising political star of Germany. Even in 1932, the Nazi Party was one of the two largest political parties in Germany.

Hitler impressed the visitors as a political leader of extreme views combined with an iron will. Little did the Schultz brothers know the role that Hitler would play in world affairs in the years ahead.

Sixtieth Anniversary Celebrated, Stamp Denied

It was February 1933, and a special celebration that was held to mark the sixtieth anniversary of the parent navel orange tree took place in Riverside. Lieutenant Governor Frank Merriam was present to speak on behalf of Jimmy Rolph, then governor.

Other dignitaries present included Frank Tetley, member of the state highway commission, and Archie D. Shamel, who read a brief history of the navel orange tree in California that spawned a great industry. The Riverside celebration of the anniversary of the first navel orange tree's planting coincided with the time of the National Orange Show in nearby San Bernardino. These celebrations helped to brighten a winter that, economically, was made grim for California and the nation by the Great Depression.

To honor the parent navel orange tree, local leaders promoted the idea of a special commemorative postage stamp to honor the tree and the Tibbets, who planted the tree and nurtured it. California senators and congressmen supported the idea of the special commemorative stamp. Congressman Phil Swing of San Bernardino was particularly aggressive in his promotion of the proposal.

The times were out of joint for the issuance of the special postage stamp. The outgoing Hoover administration deferred the matter to the incoming Franklin Roosevelt administration. The new leaders of the Post Office Department, under Postmaster General Jim Farley, were intent on issuing a commemorative stamp to honor the state of Georgia, part of what was then called the Democrats' "Solid South." The authorities felt that they could not issue two commemorative stamps in the short time allowed. The Georgia stamp had priority over the proposed navel orange tree stamp.

Congressman Swing persisted in his efforts to secure the stamp long after Riverside officials had given up on the project. The proposed stamp was never issued. Bitter comments followed the rejection of the planned stamp. Some felt that the West Coast was relegated to second place behind the interests of the East Coast. Others complained about the strong influence of southern leaders. Some called them "Bourbons" in the Democratic Party of incoming president Franklin D. Roosevelt.

Fast-forward to 2011. Recent weeks saw the issuance of a commemorative stamp to honor the lunar New Year. The brightly colored stamp shows two fruits that appear to be oranges. Actually, they are kumquats, fruit often associated with the lunar New Year in Asia. Riverside residents today can examine the lunar New Year stamp and imagine what the 1933 navel orange tree stamp would have been like seventy-eight years ago.

Dr. Ray Swain: Dentist and Much More

Many people dread dentists, and some are even hostile to them. In contrast, Ray Swain, DDS, was one of the most popular men in Riverside for more than fifty years. Swain was born in Yonkers, New York, and made his home in Riverside for many years. He was a 1927 honor student graduate of Poly High School; the all-boy school was only open for three years before it allowed girls.

Swain attended the University of Southern California's highly rated dental school, graduating in 1932 as a trained and licensed dentist. While a student at USC, he performed in the marching band, playing the coronet, and starred on the tennis team. Amateur tennis grew to be one of the loves of his life, along with his family, of course. It is reported that Ray Swain stunned the world of California tennis by defeating Ellsworth Vines in a tournament held in Ojai. This upset was probably due to a combination of Swain playing very well and Vines doing poorly that day. Vines was one of the leading California tennis players during the 1930s.

Dr. Ray Swain, a former tennis star, performed dental work on Civilian Conservation Corps laborers in Death Valley during the Depression. *Courtesy of Riverside Community College.*

In the mid-1930s, Dr. Ray Swain and his good friends John Gabbert, Norman Geibe and Dale Cunnison performed a government contract by driving to a Civilian Conservation Camp (CCC) near Death Valley, where Dr. Swain did dental work on the CCC boys. Dr. Swain had an antique portable drill powered by a stationary bicycle. The dentist's three friends took turns pumping the bicycle furiously, and the power generated drove the dental drill. Reports indicate that the dental work was performed satisfactorily, though in primitive surroundings.

The energetic young dentist joined the U.S. Army Reserves in the late 1930s as a lieutenant. When World War II came, he served in the active-duty U.S. Army, first at Camp Haan near Riverside and later in India as part of the China-Burma-India (CBI) Theater forces under overall command of British admiral Lord Mountbatten. While in India, Dr. Swain was honored at a banquet hosted by Major General and Lady Wavell. Wavell was one of the top British generals serving in the CBI Theater.

Photos sent home from India to his family by Dr. Swain show men in turbans, snake charmers with cobras, the beautiful Taj Mahal and, of course, shocking disease and widespread poverty of a kind rarely seen in the United States. Dr. Swain left the army with the rank of major after serving as both dentist and hospital administrator in India.

At home in Riverside after the war, Dr. Swain resumed his dental practice in the De Anza Theater Building. He joined the Lions Club and played tennis at every opportunity. He helped to organize tennis tournaments in cooperation with the *Riverside Press-Enterprise* and with his close friends Bob Vanderzyl and George and Clint Pooley.

Dr. Swain retired from dentistry in 1962. He practiced dentistry for fifty years here and abroad. He taught Sunday school in the Calvary Presbyterian Church. For recreation, he played tennis and golf in an active retirement. He died in December 1994 at age eighty-five. His widow, Margaret, died two years later.

MARCELLA CRAFT: TALENTED AND CRAFTY

Sarah Marcia Craft was born in Indianapolis in 1874 and moved with her family to Riverside in 1887. There her remarkable singing voice was discovered, and a group of generous businessmen paid for her trip to Boston, where she could receive the best in voice training. About the time of the Boston trip, Ms. Craft subtracted six years from her actual age. Even then, everyone in show business wanted to be younger than their actual age. One hundred years later, it was discovered that Nancy Davis Reagan had subtracted a few years from her actual age too.

Not only did Ms. Craft alter her official age, but she also changed her name. After leaving Boston, she traveled to Italy, where she became "Marcella Craft," the name she used for the rest of her life. In Italy, Marcella sang leading roles in operas, but she never felt at home there. She felt that people looked down on her as a foreigner.

She visited Germany, first on vacation and then to stay. She sang at Kiel, where she came to the attention of one of Kaiser Wilhelm's sons. With that connection and recommendation, Marcella soon became a leading lady with the Munich Opera. She was to make Munich her European home for most of her singing career. It is reputed that the composer of *Salome*, Richard Strauss, actually rewrote part of the leading role for Marcella, who had complained that she could not sing the lower range adequately.

Just as Munich was Marcella's European home, Riverside was her American home. She retired to Riverside in 1932. But "retire" was probably the wrong word, because she taught voice here and helped to organize the Riverside Opera Company. She was an active proponent of opera in English. She felt that many more people would come to enjoy opera if they could understand the words being sung on stage.

Marcella Craft never married and had no children, but she had a most interesting life. She had many friends and was quite a storyteller. In one of her anecdotes, she told of returning to Munich after World War I, where she was recognized by a streetcar conductor who had admired her from the days in Munich before the war. He refused to accept her streetcar fare.

Marcella was a woman who knew the greats of music of her time, such as Caruso, Strauss and Toscanini. In Riverside, she sang at many of the early Easter sunrise services. She was a friend of Frank Miller, master of the Mission Inn, and knew most of the art and music figures of her time in Southern California. Artists, and particularly prima donnas of opera, are renowned for their strange and demanding ways. Marcella had her eccentricities as well. One of them was that she hated to hear the sound of her singing voice on a record. Therefore, she made only one recording, or at least only one recording is known to exist.

Few people are aware of Ms. Craft's observations on the Nazis in Germany, as seen in her stay in Munich for thirty days in 1934. She spoke more than operatic German and had many friends in the southern German city of Munich. In September 1934, Ms. Craft told the Riverside Kiwanis Club that Germany was not a good place to visit at that time. The Nazis under Adolph Hitler had come to power twenty-one months earlier. She told the Kiwanis Club that she loved Germany and its people but that the politics of Germany were turbulent and difficult to understand.

She described Hitler's Nazi Party as a youth movement that had swept over Germany. Unemployment had almost ceased to exist, and there was a new spirit in the land, she related. Still, conditions in Germany were not as favorable as she had been led to believe by letters received from friends in Germany before Ms. Craft's recent trip to Munich. She offered the opinion that Hitler was a man of high ideals, but she felt that not all of his followers were as honest as he was.

As a woman, Ms. Craft noted that German women were not permitted to wear makeup and were not allowed to bob their hair. These restrictions were apparent reactions to the permissive cabaret conditions that had existed under the previous Weimar Republic.

As to the "Jewish question," Ms. Craft reported that German Jews were no longer allowed to hold government posts and that their businesses were closed for one day, presumably by government order. She added that Germans took the position that they did not want foreigners in control of the government, a situation she personally wished might prevail a bit more in America.

Marcella Craft concluded her talk to the Kiwanis Club by stating that she had great faith in the German people, expressing the belief that they would emerge from the present situation (in 1934) triumphantly. Miss Craft was not alone in admiring the early actions of the Nazi Party under Hitler in Germany. The fact that the German people had been put back to work by the German government was especially admirable to many Americans, since the United States in 1934 had high unemployment.

For many Americans in 1934, it was convenient to excuse discrimination against Jews and others because of the reduction of unemployment and German construction of such notable works as the network of autobahns. Marcella Craft, the far-ranging and greatly respected world talent, died in a Riverside nursing home in 1959 at the actual age of eighty-five.

"DESERT STEVE" RAGSDALE STUDIED AT RCC

Steven A. Ragsdale was born in Coffeeville, Kansas, in 1882 and grew up to be a Methodist minister. He did not find the ministry satisfying, so he did what many young men did: he moved west, settling in the small agricultural community of Blythe. There he almost went broke "raising six-cent cotton," as he put it.

In 1921, he moved to a seven-hundred-acre parcel in the middle of the desert located almost exactly halfway between Indio and Blythe, where he founded Desert Center. There he ran a service station and served as the lawman for the area. He was appointed deputy sheriff for three counties—Riverside, San Bernardino and Imperial. Along the way, Steve founded two other desert towns, Hell and Utopia. Neither one succeeded, and both are mere memories today.

Soon, Ragsdale was known as "Desert Steve," and he came to love the desert. The desert heat seems to produce colorful characters, as seen with Death Valley's Scotty and Harry Oliver, two of Steve's good friends. The three desert rats even developed a plan to create a state to be called Geronimo out of desert counties from Nevada, California and Arizona. This plan had zero chance of success, and the three men must have known that fact.

Next, Ragsdale and Oliver campaigned to create a desert county from the eastern half of Riverside County. Advertisements were printed showing Harry Oliver in a cowboy hat and wielding a sword while threatening to "cut the county off at the Cabazon." Though several attempts were made to cut Riverside County in half, the plans failed each time.

Desert Steve loved his desert, and he detested those who littered or damaged it. He fancied himself a poet, and he wrote warnings in verse such as this: "All decent folks welcome/ Enjoy but don't destroy." He also wrote prose. *My Friend the Tortoise* was one of his books.

Steve was married and had three sons and one daughter. He wanted a better life for his children than he had, so he sent his youngest son, Stanley, to Riverside City College (RCC). The young man did not take to college life, preferring to do "something useful," as he put it. This attitude upset Desert Steve, a man famous for his bad temper and foul language. Steve's oldest son, Thurman, challenged Steve, "Why don't you go to college?" Steve rarely backed down from a challenge, and his business was doing well in Desert Center, so Steve and his wife enrolled in Riverside City College at age fifty-three in 1935. Steve took courses in astronomy, psychology, English and philosophy.

Desert Steve loved college life. He did well in his classes and actually inspired his reluctant son, Stanley, to continue in college. Steve was in ill health during the last few years of his life. He died in 1971 at age eighty-eight. Journalists liked the crusty and profane desert rat even as he cursed at them; he was colorful and always produced good copy for publication.

BRAVE RIVERSIDE GIRL DESERVED MEDAL

In April 1937, an off-duty Riverside policeman crashed his vehicle into a palm tree on Victoria Avenue. The car immediately burst into flame, assisted by a container of volatile cleaning fluid the officer had in his car. Nearby, a young woman saw the fiery crash and the unconscious man inside the vehicle. Disregarding her own safety, she rushed to the car and pulled the unconscious policeman to safety a few seconds before the car was totally consumed by flames.

Miss Margaret Paden weighed only 105 pounds, but she managed to haul the deadweight 220-pound officer to safety. I understand that adrenalin often kicks in during crisis situations such as this one, and the adrenalin seems to add to strength. In the last few seconds of the rescue, Miss Paden was assisted by two soldiers from March Field, but it was Paden who made the lifesaving move.

Police and city officials were thrilled with the amazing "grace under pressure"—Hemingway's definition of courage—shown by the young Margaret Paden. Almost immediately, a long list of Riverside city officials and police officers wrote glowing reports of the woman's heroism and submitted them to the Carnegie Hero Fund Commission in hopes of having Miss Paden receive the Carnegie Bronze Medal. This medal is awarded to ordinary citizens who exhibit extraordinary heroism that results in a life being saved. Police and firefighters are not eligible for the medal on the theory that those individuals are paid to be heroic, and their heroism is expected in crisis situations.

The police officer in the crash was named Sergeant Dan H. Davis. He suffered a broken leg and serious burns to one side of his body, but he recovered fully thanks to the prompt efforts of Miss Paden. The injured officer was one of the poeple most insistent that Miss Paden receive the Carnegie medal for heroism. Sad to report, such was not to be. The Carnegie Hero Commission had strict requirements for the medal. It was not enough to be heroic, not enough to risk one's life in order to save another person. In addition, there had to be supporting affidavits from eyewitnesses to the heroic rescue. In the case of Margaret Paden, the only witness who could have provided a sworn statement was the policeman, who was unconscious at the time.

A terrible mine disaster in Pennsylvania in the year 1904 caused multimillionaire steel magnate Andrew Carnegie to establish the Carnegie

Hero Fund. In the year 1937, there were twelve recipients of the Carnegie Bronze Medal, but Margaret Paden was not one of them, though almost all of Riverside was convinced that she deserved the medal for risking her life in a fiery crash scene to save the life of an unconscious police officer.

The Bowleg Defense

The courtroom is normally a very serious place where laughter is rarely heard. Still, there are some cases where everyone present has to either laugh out loud or struggle to stifle a laugh.

Jim Clark was a Riverside horse trainer and former working cowboy who had been a horseman for many years. He was accused of driving his car while intoxicated in November 1938, and the jury trial was set for January 1939. Clark was arrested on Indiana Avenue after his vehicle struck a truck parked on the side of the road. Police were called, and Clark was taken to the city jail. The police physician insisted that Clark walk a straight line written in chalk as a test for intoxication. According to the doctor and arresting officers, Clark failed that test. He was jailed and ordered to face charges of drunk driving.

Clark denied the charge and hired an attorney, and the matter was set for a jury trial in the courtroom of R.A. Moore, who was a justice of the peace in Riverside from 1930 to 1953. Two big-name attorneys were involved in this trial—two men whose names were to be well known in Riverside for decades to come. Prosecuting the case as a deputy district attorney was Russell C. Waite. Waite was to become a Superior Court judge and serve in that capacity from 1947 until 1966, when he retired. For the defense, Clark hired Walter C. Davison. In 1939, he was already a well-known Riverside lawyer, and one year after the Clark trial, he was elected to serve as mayor of Riverside, serving from 1940 to 1948.

Davison's defense showed that the parked truck had no lights and that the accident took place in the darkness of night. Clark testified that he hit the truck only after swerving to avoid hitting a pedestrian. The most unusual aspect of the attorney's defense of Clark was the claim that Clark, due to his riding horseback for years, had developed bowed legs that prevented his walking a straight line. A physician hired by the defense backed up this assertion by telling the court that Clark's bowed legs would prevent his walking a straight line even if completely sober. The inability to walk a straight line was also caused by the high-heeled cowboy boots customarily worn by Clark, the doctor added. These boots were worn by Clark at the time of the arrest and the later straight-line test.

For the prosecution, Russell C. Waite relied on the failure of Clark to pass the walking test and the testimony of arresting officers. The jury mulled over the evidence presented and came to the conclusion that Jim Clark was not guilty of the charge. Clark left the courtroom a free man.

Then as now, there are persons who hang around the courthouse to view trials and discuss cases. These observers must have been astonished at the defense claims presented and, even more, that the jury accepted those claims as grounds for acquittal. The headline in the *Riverside Daily Press* article that reported the case read, "Bowlegs Free Man on Drunk Driving Trial."

LARGE CLOCKS ON MAIN STREET

Large public clocks have been present on Main Street in downtown Riverside for most of the years since 1890. The fate of those clocks, designed to aid the citizens as they sought to make their appointments, has been sometimes mysterious and sometimes dangerous.

In 1886, a group of businessmen petitioned the Riverside City Council to ask for the establishment of a clock in the tower of the Castleman Bank Building at the corner of Eighth Street (today's University Avenue) and Main Streets. The group of petitioners accumulated $430, and it asked the city to contribute $220, with the money to be used to purchase a large Seth Thomas clock. All agreed that the city would own the clock though placed in the bank building. The city council agreed, and the clock with a four-foot face was installed overlooking the principal intersection of the city. The clock had to be wound manually twice each week, and that task fell to W.E. Johnson, a local jeweler.

The clock would not only show the time but also sound the time on the hour with its bells. The main criticism of the clock was that it was often a few minutes behind the actual time. Its time lag was a mystery that no one could understand or remedy.

In 1910, the Castleman Building was demolished, and the clock was removed. For a time, it stood alone on a pedestal on Main Street. Some hoped that the clock would be installed in another downtown building. The fate of the old Seth Thomas clock is unknown. By 1915, another clock was present on Main Street. This one was on a cast-iron pedestal about fifteen feet tall. It had two large opposing faces.

Civic clocks still adorn public places in Riverside, as seen here in Arlington. The city has had mixed fortunes with them. *Photo by the author.*

On a foggy morning in January 1939, Thomas F. Bryant was driving north on Main Street when his car collided with the clock. It fell on top of Bryant's car, with the clock face showing 5:34 a.m., the time of the crash. A photo of the clock resting on the hood of Bryant's car was shown in the *Riverside Daily Press*. A reporter could not resist commenting that Bryant had "time on his hands." More accurately, time rested on the hood of his automobile.

A much more elegant four-face Seth Thomas clock had made an appearance on Main Street by the 1920s. This clock was moved several times by 1990 and was cared for by Imre Kalincsak, an expert watchmaker who owned Riverside's Swiss Clock Shop.

Some three years ago, a construction worker backed his skip loader into the large, ornate clock. The damage done was great, and some felt that it was a total loss. The worker's employer agreed to pay for the cost to repair the clock. It stands on the corner of the Main Street mall and Mission Inn Avenue. It is painted a dark green, and an observer would never guess that it had almost been destroyed in the construction accident. The restored four-face clock not only looks good, but it also keeps close to accurate time. Tony Garcia, a downtown ambassador, told me that the clock was a mere four minutes fast. He also told me that workers had been examining the clock's gears in recent days.

PERHAPS THE KIDS WERE RIGHT

For many years, beginning in the later 1930s, upperclassmen at Poly High told incoming freshmen of the swimming pool that never came to be. According to this often-told story, the city and the federal Works Progress Administration were going to cooperate in the construction of a swimming pool in Tequesquite Arroyo, not far from the football field known as Wheelock Field. Instead, the story goes, city officials diverted the funds to build the De Anza statue now at Fourteenth and Market Streets. Tom Patterson in his column of September 23, 1979, noted the long-lived legend of diverted funds but concluded that the story wasn't true.

True or not, Poly High's student body took the story as the gospel truth. The result was student resentment of the statue and the historical figure of De Anza. Some students even charged that he was an "old horse thief." I have found no evidence that he was anything but an honorable officer in the Spanish army, however.

Filled with their resentment of the statue and their desire for a swimming pool, Poly students year after year would douse the De Anza statue with

Sculptor Sherry Peticolas designed the statue of Juan Bautista de Anza, which is located at the corner Fourteenth and Market Streets in Riverside. *Photo by the author.*

paint on Halloween. Civic organizations, such as the Junior Chamber of Commerce, would get out the brushes and ladders to clean the statue. A recent discovery suggests that the kids might have been right—not about the paint, though, as I will not defend vandalism. Rather, their assertion of diversion of funds from a planned swimming pool to construction of the De Anza statue might have some truth to it.

A news article in the *Riverside Daily Press* of June 23, 1937, noted that the Riverside City Council had pledged support for a plan to build a swimming pool in the Tequesquite Arroyo for the use of Poly High and Riverside City College, then located across the Street from the high school.

The district supervisor of the Works Progress Administration indicated that the pool project met its guidelines. The plan was taken seriously enough that two council members joined several Recreation Committee members for a field trip to Ontario in order to examine the operation of the Chaffey High School pool.

No one can state for sure that the De Anza replaced the proposed swimming pool, as charged by generations of high school students. However, the pool plan was dropped, and the De Anza statue went ahead to completion in 1940, financed in part by Works Progress Administration money. With completion of the Cutter Pool in the arroyo in 1958, most of the rancor ended, but the memories remain.

Part III

World War II and Midcentury

Suicide Bomb Blast, 1942

In the middle of 1942, the United States was involved in a war that raged around the world. Here at home, there was great fear of saboteurs and unbalanced people who might damage vital installations. Frank Kritzer (sometimes spelled as Critzer) was a mystery man who lived alone on a dry lake called Giant Rock in the desert north of Twentynine Palms.

Kritzer was suspected of having Nazi sympathies. He had set off some flares, and the army feared that they might constitute a signal to spies in hiding. In addition, he had a high-powered radio with a four-hundred-foot-high aerial. Kritzer had been under observation by the Federal Bureau of Investigation (FBI), military intelligence and the sheriffs of both Riverside and San Bernardino Counties. He was suspected of stealing hundreds of pounds of dynamite and hiding the loot in his home, which he had hollowed out of a rock in the desert.

Kritzer had earned a living by selling visiting pilots food, gasoline and other material supplies at his airstrip on the dry lake of Giant Rock. When war came, civilian flying was curtailed, and he had little income. The little he had came from tourists who paid to tour his unique home cut out of a large rock.

In July 1942, three deputy sheriffs visited the rock home to arrest Kritzer for the alleged theft of dynamite. The suspect was determined not to be taken away. He met the officers with a binocular case around his neck. Inside the case he had placed dynamite. When the officers approached, Kritzer set off the dynamite. The explosion blew him to bits and caused serious injuries to Deputy Sheriff C.F. McCracken but only superficial injuries to his two fellow officers. Inside the rock home there was a pile of dynamite of up to two hundred pounds. If Kritzer's explosion had set off that pile of dynamite, as he had intended, all three deputies would have been killed along with Kritzer.

Possibly the loss of income and the isolation of his life coupled with the desert heat had unhinged Kritzer's mind. In 1942, suicide bombers were most unusual. One press account of the incident termed the explosion "one of the weirdest suicides on record." This report indicates that, long before the development of plastic explosives and long before the rise of militant Islam, there was, even in inland Southern California, at least one fatal suicide bombing caused by explosives.

In this 1942 incident, all three of the Riverside County deputy sheriffs survived their injuries caused by the suicide bomber. In the months and years following 2001, Americans (civilian and military) have not always been so fortunate.

There is another point to this story. A policeman or sheriff never knows what will be the reaction of the person about to be arrested, or even questioned, by the authorities. Most of the time, the officer can expect and receive citizen cooperation. But now and then, the actions of desperate individuals may be harmful, or even fatal, to others.

Officer of Camp Haan

Bill H. McGaugh is ninety years old, alert and spry. He chuckled as he claimed to be "the last of the Mohicans." He was referring to his claim to be the last surviving army officer to have served at Camp Haan, a World War II U.S. Army base located across the highway from March Field. The army camp stretched for three miles along that highway and housed eighty thousand soldiers at its peak.

During the war, Bill served as assistant to the commanding general of the training command at Camp Haan. Bill rose from private to sergeant to warrant officer during the course of the war. In his position, he was in touch with most of the everyday problems on the base. He was able to end the wastage of food. Cooks were cooking for the number of men assigned rather than for the number actually present. He questioned the army's standard menu, which included hominy grits. Troops from the South liked grits, but those from the North did not. Having served as both an enlisted man and as an officer, Bill stated firmly that officers ate much better meals than the troops.

Bill recalled that San Bernardino was considered a center of vice by the army, so soldiers were forbidden to enter some sections of that city. Military police patrolled the streets where brothels were known to exist. Bill had more than one hundred women working for him at Camp Haan. Most were secretaries and clerical workers. He laughed as he recalled that the women were very popular with the many soldiers in camp.

Contrary to expectations, most of the troops from Camp Haan were sent to the European Theater of Operations rather than to the Pacific Theater. The big guns of the artillery were of more use in the land campaigns of Europe than in the island-hopping of the Pacific war.

Today, the area of the former Camp Haan is divided between vacant land, the National Cemetery and the General Olds Golf Course. Bill stated that the Camp Haan headquarters building was located precisely where the cemetery office is today. When asked if he ever considered making the army his career, Bill replied, "No, I did not like the military way of doing things."

After leaving the army, Bill and his wife, Beverly, settled in Riverside. He entered the retail paint business. Now retired for the second time, Bill looks forward to each new day. He recently returned from a cruise to Australia and New Zealand. He joked that his ship captain was not Italian. Bill lost his wife a while back. He is planning future trips with his new lady friend. He lives on the seventh floor of Plymouth Towers on Lemon Street where his view of downtown Riverside is spectacular.

He attended Riverside Junior College in the days before entering the army, and he is a generous donor to RCC causes. He is active in the Riverside Optimist Club and proudly lists the activities sponsored by the club. These activities include college scholarships and the Tri-Star Basketball Tournament. Bill is also justly proud of his two adult daughters. Marcia is a psychotherapist, and Bonnie has degrees in both anthropology and interior design.

If there is another living army officer who served during World War II at Camp Haan, Bill does not know of that person. If he is not "Last of the Mohicans," he must be one of the very few surviving officers from that time in camp. He was recently interviewed in the studio of the University of California–Riverside. This interview was arranged by Media Supervisor Jim Brown. The video program will be an aid to future historians of the military in the Riverside area.

Two Riverside Navy Brothers Perished

For Veterans Day, it is fitting that we honor our servicemen and servicewomen. Two brothers grew up in Riverside and became senior officers in the U.S. Navy. As naval aviators, they died in separate accidents involving a U.S. Navy aircraft carrier.

Grady Weeks graduated from Poly High in 1946. He joined the navy and became an aviator. He also was the navy's first doctoral candidate in solid state physics. This brilliant scientist was seen as one of Defense Secretary McNamara's "Whiz Kids." When Grady returned to the fleet air arm, he was assigned to fly the F-4 with VF 161 in the carrier USS *Constellation* (CV-64).

Flying a hot jet plane off an aircraft carrier is a most dangerous occupation, and landing such a plane at night is even more dangerous. On an attempted night landing while the carrier was en route to Vietnam in May 1966, Commander Grady Weeks crashed his plane and was killed. The nation lost not only a fine naval aviator but also a promising scientist.

Younger brother Dennis Weeks also grew up in Riverside, graduating from Poly High in 1953. He attended both Riverside Community College and University of California–Riverside. At UCR, Dennis was elected student body president in 1958. Dennis followed his older brother into the navy and into naval aviation. Dennis completed flight training and entered the fleet as an officer and as an aviator, just as Grady had done. Dennis rose through the ranks to become commander, the equivalent of lieutenant colonel in the army or air force, and was assigned to the aircraft carrier USS *Midway* (CV-41), the same carrier that is now a museum in San Diego Harbor.

In a second tragedy, Commander Dennis Weeks attempted a takeoff from the USS *Midway*, and he suffered what the navy calls a "cold cat." That means that the catapult shot designed to launch the heavy aircraft into the air was inadequate, and the plane crashed into the sea. Dennis Weeks was killed in that crash, which took place in August 1975.

In the two tragedies, Grady Weeks was killed in an attempted carrier landing, and Dennis Weeks was killed in an attempted takeoff. Dennis was flying a twin-engine A-6 attack plane. For those who are superstitious, the Weeks brothers grew up in the home formerly located at 3368 Thirteenth Street, Riverside. Years after the Weeks family left the home, sometime in 2000, that house was destroyed by fire.

The deaths of the Weeks brothers serve to remind us that men and women lose their lives in accidents as well as in combat. Memorial Day is a time to specifically remember these brave members of the armed forces who have died in the service of their country.

Thanks go to Rear Admiral Allen Hill (USN-Ret.) and Commander Kirk Ferguson (USN-Ret.) for their contributions to this section. Admiral Hill was a classmate of Grady Weeks at Poly High, class of 1946. Commander Ferguson was a classmate of Dennis Weeks, Poly High class of 1953.

FUSELAGE FOR A HOME

Probably the most unusual home in Riverside is an airplane fuselage located at the extreme western end of Rubidoux Avenue. The home is an old cargo transport airplane, minus the wings and tail sections. The fuselage is pointed toward the west to provide a view of the Santa Ana River floodplain and Rubidoux to the west from the cockpit.

In the days right after World War II, housing in Riverside was in short supply, and building materials were expensive. Two young women purchased a war surplus C-46 transport plane. They removed wings and tail structure and moved the fuselage to its present location on Rubidoux Avenue. It has been there since 1947.

The body of the aircraft was placed on a concrete foundation. Insulation was added along with utilities to the home. A kitchenette was placed in the tail of the fuselage, and two large bedrooms were placed forward. At first, there were no closets, but the fuselage contains two large storage compartments that form a basement to the living spaces.

The two daring female owners called their unusual home the "Confusi-Lodge." They did most of the work on the project themselves. The two owners came from very different backgrounds but had formed a lasting friendship. Cheryl Williams was a disabled former navy officer, and Jean

Behind the cacti and the trailer is the fuselage home. The airplane was a Curtiss-Wright C-46. *Photo by the author.*

Sutherland was notable as a golfer. She was the daughter of Mrs. Hazel Sutherland, owner of Sutherland's Coffee Shop on Main Street in 1947.

As seen today, the fuselage appears to be in good condition. The original silver color has been maintained. An air vent has been added on top of the fuselage to promote cooling of the interior. A wooden stairway bridges the gap from the ground to the door of the plane's body. The yard around the aircraft home is fenced, and this writer has not been able to see the interior of the home. Letters addressed to the owner of record of the property have not been answered.

Material in this column is based on observation from the street outside the property, plus information contained in an article dated January 4, 1947, in the *Riverside Daily Press*. The article described the two women and their adaptation of the military aircraft to a unique home.

It is unlikely that the owner of the unusual home realizes the treasure he has. There is a similar airplane fuselage fitted out as a hotel room in Puerto Quepos, Costa Rica. That fuselage hotel room overlooks a jungle canopy, and it rents for $400 to $500 per night, depending on seasonal demand.

PARKING METERS IN RIVERSIDE

Recently I read a book titled *History's Worst Inventions* by Eric Chaline. It was surprising to me that the parking meter was not listed as one of the worst. True, the meter is not as terrible as poison gas or the electric chair, but it is detested by many motorists. The parking meter was patented by an Oklahoma City man named Carl C. Magee in 1935. Within weeks, it was put in place in cities across the land.

The Riverside Chamber of Commerce called for installation of parking meters downtown in the late 1930s, but the meters were put not in place downtown until the late 1940s. Those opposed charged that downtown would look like a cemetery with the meters resembling tall tombstones. Tombstones or not, the meters were installed. A 1949 photo shows them on Main Street in front of Rouse's Department Store.

With the parking meters came the meter maids, who wrote tickets for those who had overstayed their metered time. Riverside's meter maids were so efficient that the City of Santa Ana sent several trainees to learn from the

Parking meters—the new (left) and the old—have been the bane of many shoppers and other visitors but have provided the City of Riverside with vital income. *Photo by the author.*

Riverside crew. Some Riverside drivers claimed bitterly that the meter maids formed the most efficient unit of the City of Riverside.

As downtown Riverside declined in the early and mid-1960s, some blamed the parking meters. Shopping centers such as the Riverside Plaza and Hardman Center offered ample free parking and the absence of those vigilant meter maids.

In 1950, a penny would buy twelve minutes of time on the Riverside meter. Today, the rate is one dollar per hour. The complexity of meters rose along with price. Dan Bernstein, a popular columnist for the *P-E*, reported a few years ago that a UCR professor with a PhD from Harvard University was confused and mystified by the meter then in use. The meters have become far more complicated since that time. A new model meter in use is solar powered, and just one costs the city $10,000. With complexity comes the tendency to break down. We will never know how many motorists were ticketed due to a malfunctioning meter.

For months, perhaps years, downtown streets had signs that read "Pay Here." A visitor to Riverside might have concluded that "Pay Here" was the city motto. A more modest circled "P" has replaced the blatant demand for funds.

There are alternatives to the parking meter, that voracious gobbler of cash. Parking on Saturday or Sunday is free at the meter. There are two parking garages on Orange Street between Mission Inn Avenue and Ninth Street that offer free parking for ninety minutes any day of the week. A new parking garage has been built on Market Street next to the Fox Theater that will house four hundred cars.

Though many hate parking meters and insist that they have contributed to the decline of downtown and the creation of urban sprawl, there is an opposing view. Professor Donald Sharp of UCLA pointed out that Old Town Pasadena was revived from a blighted area when meters were installed.

Love them or loathe them, it appears that parking meters are in downtown Riverside to stay. It is interesting that not one of the cities that borders Riverside has parking meters. Not Corona, not San Bernardino and not Pomona. The meters are also not found in commercial areas of Riverside other than downtown. There are no meters on the streets of Magnolia Center or Arlington.

Money doesn't just talk; it *screams*. The meters brought in $1.4 million in 2010.

The Policemen's Ball, 1949

Do you ever wish you could go back in time for a day or for a special event? If you were granted such a wish, the fifteenth annual Policemen's Ball of 1949 would be a great Riverside event to wish for. The ball was held on Saturday evening, November 5, 1949, in the downtown Riverside Municipal Auditorium on Mission Inn Avenue (then Seventh Street).

Retired Riverside police captain Bill St. Marie still recalls one of the balls. Tickets to the event were shaped like police badges, and officers wore fancy blue dress uniforms complete with black Sam Browne belts. Jimmie Grier and his orchestra provided dance music for the crowd on the main floor. In the basement of the auditorium, Art Wenzel's Ragtime Cowboys offered western music with a jazz beat. Riverside resident Eddie Peabody, known as "King of the Banjo," was so popular that the crowd insisted on his playing number after number.

Hoagy Carmichael, composer of "Stardust," was in Riverside to benefit the Policemen's Ball. He performed many of his hits and other selections on the piano. Finally, there was a magician billed as "the Great Trudini." He was called a "Magician Extraordinary."

Admission to this all-star program, which went on till the wee hours, was one dollar per person. While it is true that one dollar bought far more in

Eddie Peabody was known as the "King of the Banjo." He owned a citrus ranch in Riverside, and his home still stands. *From the author's collection.*

1949 than it buys today, the Policemen's Ball was still a big bargain—one fine night's entertainment for one dollar. Press reviews of the evening were more than favorable. They were enthusiastic. The review in the *Daily Press* bore the headline, "Everybody Turns Out for the Annual Policemen's Ball." It was truth in advertising when the print ads for the 1949 Policemen's Ball proclaimed, "Never Before So Much for So Little!" Sponsors of newspaper advertisements for the 1949 ball were Bradley-Rehrig, an army-navy surplus store, and Stockwell-Binney, a stationery store.

The annual Riverside Policemen's Ball tradition came to an end in the mid-1950s. The Riverside firemen also had annual balls, and the last Firemen's Ball was held in May 1955. The Firemen's Ball is a story for another day and another page.

Charles of London versus the Oak Tree

Should a large oak tree be considered a city treasure or a hindrance to commerce? That issue came before the Riverside City Council in the autumn of 1949, with strange, contradictory results.

The large oak was located at 6623 Magnolia Avenue, on the west side of Magnolia between Jurupa Avenue and the railroad tracks. According to beauty shop owner Charles of London, the presence of the large oak in front of his business made it difficult for his customers to enter and exit the business. Charles demanded the tree be removed. The next-door neighbor was insurance man Austin Howell, who treasured the oak for its shade and beauty. He opposed removal of the tree.

The issue went to the Riverside City Park Board, and the board investigated and issued a recommendation to the city council that the tree be maintained in place. The city council overruled the park and tree board by voting to permit Charles to remove the tree. But before removal could take place, Austin Howell made an appeal to the council.

Citrus Experiment Station scientist and tree lover Archie D. Shamel addressed the city council with these words: "Trees are defenseless. Someone has to defend them, and I am here to do it." He praised the shade-giving virtue of the huge tree. He emphasized that it takes many years to grow such a large and noble oak. Howell told the council that the tree was more on his land than on Charles's land. City inspectors backed up Howell's claim.

Police Chief J.A. Bennett told the council and the crowd assembled that Charles's driveway could be made safe without removing the oak.

Charles came back with the promise to provide Howell with two trees if permitted to remove the single oak. When the offer was refused, Charles promised that he would widen his driveway "even if the tree gets hurt." After hearing all of the testimony, the city council voted four to one to reverse itself and to deny Charles permission to take out the tree. Councilman Zollie Hair was the lone holdout in favor of tree removal.

More than sixty years ago in Riverside, in a small way, the issue of business desires versus environmental concerns was addressed and readdressed by the city council. The issue has come up many times since 1949, with business interests winning some of the battles and environmentalists winning others. It is safe to predict that such issues will reappear in Riverside and in other cities again and again as time goes by.

BOB HOPE IN COMMUNITY HOSPITAL

Comedian Bob Hope has had several contacts with Riverside, beginning with his frequent trips from Los Angeles to Palm Springs. Soon after American entry into World War II, Hope organized his troupe of Hollywood entertainers to bring joy to the troops. His first place to present his act was Riverside's March Field.

Hope often stayed at the Mission Inn, where his wild humor must have shaken the stiff decorum of the staff in the 1940s. Hope presented at least one radio program from Riverside's Memorial Auditorium. Passing to and from the big city to Palm Springs, Hope would often stop to buy gas or grab a meal. Seeing the unmistakable face of the comedian would give some workers something to talk about for days.

On a rainy night in January 1950, Hope was driving from Palm Springs to his home in Los Angeles when he lost control of the car and swerved off the Highway 60 about sixteen miles east of Riverside. The car overturned, and Hope and his writer, Fred Williams, found themselves injured and in mud up to their ankles. A passing motorist saw the situation and gave Hope and his companion a ride to Riverside's Community Hospital. The physician on duty at the hospital treated Hope for a dislocated shoulder. Williams had an injured leg. Neither injury was considered to be serious, and both were soon released.

Bob Hope was once hospitalized in Riverside following an auto accident. *Courtesy of Steve Takata.*

Newspapermen and a photographer were soon on the scene. They were not disappointed. Hope rewarded them with one of his many jokes. "Of course I am fine," he reported. "I have just had a mud bath on Highway 60." As Hope was wheeled out of the emergency room on a gurney, a door accidentally banged the back of the gurney. That resulted in another Hope joke. "Boy, you guys almost did it that time. This is my unlucky day."

Weather conditions in and near the Badlands were bad that January day. The rain had made the road slick and dangerous. A second car swerved off the road and into a ditch the same day that Hope's vehicle overturned. In another wisecrack, Hope suggested that the county was cooperating with Pierce Brothers, a Los Angeles mortuary, in its maintenance of the highway. Neither one of the biographies of Bob Hope that I consulted mentioned the crash near Riverside. It was a small incident in the life of the entertainer but a big thing in Riverside to those who saw Hope and heard him.

Later, Bob Hope's generous nature resulted in several important contributions to Riverside County. He donated eighty acres of land to the Eisenhower Medical Center in Rancho Mirage. His Bob Hope Celebrity Golf Tournament produced millions for desert cities' charities.

Bob Hope and his wife, Dolores, won the Coachella Valley Humanitarian Award in February 1984. It has often been written that Hope was one of the wealthiest of the Hollywood stars and one of the most generous to charities of all types. He died in 2003 at age 100, and Dolores followed him in death at age 102 in 2011.

THE ANDY GUMP MURDER TRIAL

In November 1952, the charge of first-degree murder resulted in a sensational Riverside trial. John Chauncey Lawrance, age thirty-seven, was accused of murdering his sixteen-year-old niece, Kathryn Knodel, with a blunt instrument. Lawrance pleaded not guilty and also not guilty by virtue of insanity. The insanity plea was eliminated when two psychiatrists from Patton State Hospital testified, after examining him, that the accused was sane. Lawrance had a prominent nose and a receding chin, so observers and the press called him "Andy Gump" after the cartoon character he was said to resemble.

The jury of eight women and four men was selected to hear the case in Judge John Gabbert's Superior Court in downtown Riverside. Assistant District Attorney Elwood Rich was chosen by District Attorney William Mackey to present the case for the prosecution. Defense attorney William Shaw of Riverside was selected to present the defense argument before the jury.

The victim had been bludgeoned to death on a road near Cherry Valley. Lawrance admitted that he previously had sexual relations with his niece. He claimed that he was in the process of changing a tire on his car when the jack slipped, injuring the girl's head severely. Lawrance could not find a pulse, so he panicked. He beat her head with a rock to make it appear that she was the victim of a hit-and-run accident. Then he disposed of the body on a road near Palm Springs.

Medical doctor and Loma Linda professor of pathology Dr. John Roos testified that no one blow killed the girl. Rather, he said, she had been beaten to death by many blows with a blunt instrument. Both Lawrance's mother and father testified on behalf of Lawrance, claiming that he was a man of good character and incapable of such acts as charged. The prosecuting attorney, Rich, brought in as evidence a certified copy of a felony conviction from Los Angeles County. Lawrance had earlier denied that he had ever been convicted of a felony.

The trial was marked by at least two surprises. In one, Deputy District Attorney Rich was elected to the Municipal Court as judge, so he had to step down as lead prosecutor. William Mackey, the county's district attorney, stepped in to finish the prosecution's case.

Second, and more tragically, one of the jurors, Earl Ainsworth, age seventy-two, suffered a heart attack in the courtroom and died. This event caused Judge Gabbert to discontinue court proceedings for the remainder of the day. An alternate juror was seated to replace the deceased, and the trial continued the next day.

The verdict of guilty was reached after only one hour and eight minutes of jury deliberation. Lawrance was not only found guilty, he was given the death penalty for the first-degree murder conviction. The California Supreme Court affirmed the Riverside County verdict, and Lawrance was executed in the gas chamber at San Quentin as directed by law.

Joe W. Rice, Colorful Sheriff

Joe Warren Rice was the type of man a casting director would choose to play a western sheriff in a movie. He was big, blunt and outspoken, and he loved firearms. He often dressed in western attire. Rice was born in Anson, Texas, in 1908 and attended public schools before working nine years for a company in Fort Worth. Beginning in 1936, he became a police officer in that city. He attended law school at night and passed the Texas Bar examination to become a lawyer.

Still eager to improve himself, Rice took courses in law enforcement and administration at Texas Christian University. In 1942, he became a special agent of the FBI and was assigned to work in various cities across the land. In January 1946, Rice was transferred to Riverside as resident agent of the FBI.

When Sheriff Carl Rayburn retired in October 1952, the Riverside Board of Supervisors chose Rice to be the eighth sheriff of Riverside County. Rice was even more active as sheriff than he had been as a policeman and law student in Texas. He joined a long list of organizations in Riverside, from Elks and Moose to the Boy Scouts and Shriners.

In the eleven years Rice served as sheriff, he made a few enemies. This active man made no secret of his strong anti-Communist feelings and conservative political views. He brought to Riverside the film *Operation Abolition*, which he showed to the public at Landis Auditorium in 1961. The film showed strong support for the House Unamerican Activities Committee and its actions. Its showing was marred by boos and demonstrations from viewers who felt that the film was biased and that the committee shown was in constant violation of American civil rights.

The sheriff had frequent disagreements with the Riverside County Board of Supervisors and was a strong opponent of all gambling proposals made in the county. One of Sheriff Rice's most vocal opponents was Riverside Community College instructor Cecil Johnson, who accused the sheriff of "trying to impose censorship" on news and magazines with his anti-pornography drive. Johnson also faulted Rice with involving himself in the "ideological beliefs" of people in Riverside County.

Still, the public seemed to approve of Joe Rice's policies as sheriff. In his third bid for reelection, in 1962, Rice won with fifty-two thousand votes, and his four opponents had a total of twenty-four thousand votes. Long before Maricopa County, Arizona, produced Sheriff Joe Arpaio, the sheriff who issued his inmates pink underwear, Riverside County had a milder version in this outspoken, active western sheriff. Joe Rice worked hard at being sheriff of Riverside County, often putting in sixteen-hour workdays. Perhaps his hard work and dedication to the position were factors contributing to his early death. Sheriff Rice died while still in office one day before his fifty-fifth birthday in 1963. He left his wife, Louise. The Rices had no children.

ROSE MARIE, WHERE ARE YOU?

Rose Marie Birdsall was an attractive waitress convicted of involuntary manslaughter in the bludgeoning of her brother-in-law in an emotional trial held in the San Bernardino Superior Court in 1951. The judge gave her a one- to ten-year sentence, and she was sent to the California Institute for Women at Tehachapi in Kern County. Even then, there was an effort to soften the name of the state's only prison for women by calling it the "Institution for Women." Perhaps it was chivalry. Prison, lawmakers thought, was for hardened criminals such as John Dillinger, Al Capone and Machine Gun Kelly. Females deserved better, in name if not in comforts.

Birdsall, age twenty-six, escaped from the institution at Tehachapi. Like most prison escapees, she was promptly recaptured. In 1952, a sharp earthquake destroyed most of the prison at Tehachapi, and the inmates were transferred to the new California Institution for Women near Norco. Note that the genteel description outlasted the prison at Tehachapi to continue at the new facility, which for many years was listed as being in Frontera. In early 1953, the Frontera facility was not yet complete when the convicts arrived. Rose Marie saw her opportunity in the construction confusion and escaped prison for the second time. This time she had a companion, a convicted forger.

The warden of the institution explained to the press that the escape of the two women would not have occurred had the facility not been in disarray due to construction. This statement by the warden completely ignored the earlier escape made by Ms. Birdsall from the Tehachapi institution, which had not yet been destroyed by earthquake. Prison officials are often reluctant to give credit to the ingenuity of escaped convicts.

Most convicts, male or female, who escape custody are recaptured within days, often within hours. In the case of Ms. Birdsall, she and her fellow escapee were found in a motel in Monterey Park after nine days. The two convicts had registered as two sisters from Seattle. On the registration form, they had mistakenly placed Seattle in California.

Ms. Birdsall had dyed her hair red. The two escapees had less than $2 between them, though a former boyfriend had given them $100, according to Ms. Birdsall's companion, the forger. The two women were arrested on charges of escape and returned to the California Institution for Women. During her stay at CIW prior to her second escape, Ms. Birdsall had been described as a "troublemaker."

Ms. Birdsall, prisoner no. 1579-A, was released from CIW in 1962 and apparently went straight after that date. She has not been returned to a California prison or to an institution for women. If Rose Marie Birdsall is alive today, she would be in her mid-eighties. Her whereabouts are unknown.

In conclusion, this writer must express some admiration for the remarkable woman whose escapes from two California prisons were both daring and successful, at least for a few days. A female convict who escapes prison once is a rarity. To escape twice is most unusual.

Thanks go to both the Claremont Public Library and Lieutenant Felix Figueroa of CIW for information used in this section.

Poly High Teacher Enriched Lives

In every profession, there is someone who is recognized as the best in his or her field. William Marvin Bell III was recognized as the finest instructor in English at Riverside's Poly High School for many years.

Bell was the son of teachers. He grew up in Los Angeles and attended UCLA on a U.S. Navy ROTC scholarship. He graduated just in time for World War II, and he served in the South Pacific as a Marine Corps officer. He received the Purple Heart for a wound suffered in combat. After the war, Bell returned to his first love: teaching high school English and literature.

Bell was colorful. Sometimes he would act out swordplay while on top of his desk. He delighted in telling his students about the gooney birds on Midway Island. Commander Kirk Ferguson, a retired naval officer and a former student, recalled that "Mr. Bell had a talent for making his English classes interesting."

Bell dominated the classroom and, though demanding, was very popular with his students. He was alive, adventurous and forward-looking. He had a strong message for his male students: "There is nothing unmanly about loving good literature."

In 1952, the Poly High yearbook, the *Koala*, described him as "the erudite William Bell III, of the gleaming eye and bristling wit. He taught his classes everything, including English." This is high tribute, indeed, from high school students taking a course required for graduation.

Bill Bell retired from full-time teaching after almost forty years at Poly High, but that was not the end of his teaching. He volunteered to be an unpaid teacher's aide at several Riverside schools. Throughout his career, Bell made his home available to boys, especially to those without father figures. At Bell's place, boys could box, fence and listen to Bell expound on guns, war and much more.

After World War II, Bell stayed in the Marine Corps Reserve, and he rose to the rank of lieutenant colonel. Bell was an outstanding teacher, a warrior and, most of all, an enthusiastic and helpful human being. He died in 2000 at age eighty-three and was mourned by family and the many appreciative students whose lives he had enriched through the years.

Round Raceway Revived in Corona

Almost everyone loves a free, open-air festival, and when that festival includes antique cars, varied food, a parade and an auto race, the festival is almost irresistible.

On Memorial Day 1953, the city of Corona staged a retrospective race, complete with a parade and horseless carriages. By one definition, a horseless carriage is an auto built before 1920. The purpose of this Corona festival was to celebrate an important part of that city's history: the auto races that were held on Corona's circular road, Grand Avenue, early in the last century.

The races were held in 1913, 1914 and 1916. The race cars of the period roared around the one-mile-diameter Grand Avenue at speeds that exceeded one hundred miles per hour. And this was at a time when "mile a minute" (sixty miles per hour) was considered fast. Those races included such famous race car drivers as Eddie Rickenbacker, Barney Oldfield and Ralph DePalma.

The 1916 race was the last of the races on Corona's circular avenue. A race car driven by Bob Burman crashed, killing the driver, a mechanic and a spectator. Already in 1916, race cars were too fast for the unfenced circular roadway.

Ralph DePalma was still around and healthy in 1953. He had raced in all three of the early Corona races around Grand Avenue. His wife was chosen to be the grand marshal of the 1953 parade and festival. Some of the horseless carriages that proceeded slowly in the parade included such long-gone makes as Star, Premier and Panhard. Adding to the old-time flavor, tickets to participate in the race and parade were exact replicas of those from 1916. There was a race around Grand Avenue featuring sports cars from the 1950s that produced a victory for the Jaguar over the MG.

Four bands participated in the parade, including units from Bellflower and Beaumont, as well as bands from the two Corona high schools of the time. A comical parade entry featured two men in a bathtub with a woman, under a parasol, looking on in astonishment.

The race and parade were televised nationally, and Fox Movietone News, a newsreel company, took film for showing in theaters across the land. After the race around the Grand Avenue circle and the parade, the cars from two very different eras were placed on display in a nearby park for all to examine up close, although "look but don't touch" was the rule.

History, automobiles old and new, a parade and a picnic all combined to provide a memorable day for Corona and for the estimated 100,000 people who gathered to view the show.

JAMES STRINGFELLOW: VILLAIN OR PAWN?

For many months, James Stringfellow was probably the most hated and reviled man in western Riverside County. If he had to leave his name at a restaurant, he would use "String" instead of his actual name because people glared at him and even insulted him when he was correctly identified.

In the early 1950s, the Stringfellow Quarry Company cut and dynamited rocks out of the Jurupa Mountain on Pyrite to extract rock for jetties and breakwaters along the coast at Long Beach and Los Angeles Harbors. In 1955, a group of officials connected with the California state government went to Stringfellow to propose that he use the quarry site for a toxic waste dump. He told the officials no. He was not interested. They returned to the quarry later that year with a larger offer and told him that the canyon where the seventeen-acre quarry was located was the ideal spot for the waste dump.

A geologist was hired to make an investigation, and he assured one and all that the solid bedrock would prevent the spread of acids and toxic materials into the groundwater. All of the dangerous materials would be contained, the geologist promised. Later, investigators learned that the geologic survey was done quickly and cheaply. It cost only $300 and was completed within forty minutes. No drilling or exploration of underlying rock or earth was made. Stringfellow agreed to the plan, and the operation came to be known as the Stringfellow Acid Pits.

Almost from the beginning, the dump leaked and polluted the water table beneath the pits and for an ever-increasing distance down Pyrite Avenue. An underground lake of polluted water stretched for at least two miles south of the former quarry.

Residents of the area complained of rashes and other ailments, even when they no longer drank well water from near the acid pits. Residents could not sell their homes since everyone had heard about the pollution stream beneath them. The acid pits were closed in 1972, but the damage had been done. The Stringfellow Acid Pits were called the "Love Canal of the West" after the heavily polluted area near Niagara Falls, New York. Years later, a toxic cleanup began that has cost $120 million and is still rising in cost.

Stringfellow and his family were reviled and ridiculed. It was hard to escape the burden of his distinctive family name. He moved to Orange County, first to Newport Beach and later to Costa Mesa. He spent his final years cleaning and painting the hulls of pleasure boats in Newport Harbor.

Poor Stringfellow was duped. He believed that the geologist whose superficial report promised no toxic waste spillover into the groundwater. True, he was persuaded to sell by the amount of money offered, but he had no idea of the damage that was to follow his sale of the quarry.

Even Penny Newman, leader of the activists determined to clean up the toxic mess, was quoted as saying, "I always thought the Stringfellow family was as much a victim in this situation as anyone else."

James B. Stringfellow died in July 1993 at age sixty-six.

The People v. Felicitas Nicholson

The longest criminal trial in Riverside County history (six weeks) as of 1958 began following the discovery of young Heidi Nicholson's body in the Casa Contenta Motel on East Eighth Street, today's University Avenue. One day later, the mother of the five-year-old child was found on the beach at Long Beach. She was dazed and incoherent. Blood was found on her clothing. The mother, a thirty-two-year-old German war bride, was arrested and charged with the murder of her daughter.

Mrs. Felicitas Nicholson entered a dual plea: not guilty and not guilty by reason of insanity. The trial was not only long, it was emotional, and it seemed to include a most influential cast of characters. There was even a "mystery witness" who added little to the case.

E. Scott Dales, the public defender assigned to defend Mrs. Nicholson, was the son of Riverside mayor E.V. Dales. Dales was assisted by Deputy John Morgan. The jury foreman in this case was retired brigadier general James T. Loome of Riverside. A total of fifty-six witnesses were called, and seventy-four items were offered into evidence.

The judge in the case was John Gabbert, who had served on the Superior Court in Riverside for eight years at the time of the trial. Judge Gabbert permitted *Daily Press* photographer Fred Bauman to take photos in the courtroom during the trial under strict conditions. More traditional judges in Sacramento criticized Judge Gabbert for his decision, but the decision set a precedent, and soon other courts were permitting in-court photos. Later, Judge Gabbert was promoted to the California District Court of Appeals. That elevation took place in 1970.

The Nicholson trial was held in the main Riverside courthouse, and it attracted a full courtroom of spectators each day. They were given a show worthy of a Perry Mason television drama. Witnesses described the fatal injuries inflicted on the child, including lacerations that exposed the skull bone and crushed ribs, that suggested that the killer had jumped up and down on the child's body. Mrs. Nicholson, a pretty brunette, called out in court, "You lie," in response to a witness who testified. The accused woman wept many times during the course of the trial.

A former employer testified that Mrs. Nicholson had often displayed angry and emotional outbursts on the job. At least twice before the killing, she had been taken to the County General Hospital for observation following public screaming. Once she had attempted suicide. There was testimony that she had been wounded and traumatized in the bombing during the last stages of World War II in her native Germany. She testified that she had been raped by Russian soldiers after Germany's defeat.

In the first trial, the jury found her guilty of murder in the first degree. The second trial resulted in the death penalty. However, two psychiatrists from Patton State Hospital found that she was insane, so Judge Gabbert sentenced her to Patton until she regained sanity.

After more than seven years in Patton, she was found to be sane and released. She returned to Riverside, where Judge Gabbert vacated the murder conviction, reduced the crime to involuntary manslaughter and placed her on ten years' probation. She chose to live in Riverside with friends.

One of the curious facts about this long, emotional case is that Judge John Gabbert, while a student at Riverside Junior College, had witnessed part of the 1928 Northcott trial, another shocking, sensational and grisly murder case tried in the Riverside County Courthouse.

First Jail Break and Consequences

The Riverside County Jail had been in existence for thirty-six years before the first successful jail break was made in December 1958. Somehow, two convicts acquired a hacksaw and cut through soft metal bars in the first stage of their escape. Then they made their way to the roof of the jail building and lowered themselves to the ground by using a makeshift rope ladder made of jail bedding.

The two prisoners were Richard C. Skinner, then twenty-nine, and James E. Holloway, then twenty-six. Skinner had been sentenced to one year in jail for burglary. He had only four months to serve before completing his sentence. Holloway had been sentenced to one year in jail for failure to provide for his wife. He also faced charges of forgery in San Bernardino County.

Both escapees had criminal records dating back seven years, according to Sheriff's Captain Carl Forsteneau. Both escapees had been trusty prisoners in the county jail, and both had privileges denied to other inmates in the jail. Detective Sergeant Lawrence Brooks told the press, "We've checked every lead and had no luck, but we will get them eventually."

That prediction soon came true, at least as to Skinner, whom sheriffs considered the leader of the two escapees. Five days after the reported escape, Skinner was arrested in San Diego. He had asked his half-brother for money, and the man did not want to part with the cash; he also did not want to be seen as assisting an escapee from jail. The half-brother notified the police, who promptly arrested Skinner.

One of the most unusual aspects of the whole strange case was Skinner's reaction upon being returned to Riverside. Skinner told sheriff's deputies that he was embarrassed because jail personnel had been decent and had treated him fairly. Skinner felt bad because he had wronged them.

Skinner's partner in the escape, James Holloway, was captured in Norwalk six days after his escape. Like Skinner, he admitted that he was embarrassed and regretted harming the reputation of the jailers. A most unusual conclusion of this strange case came when an assistant jailer named Herbert Clark Card, then forty-three, admitted that he had given the hacksaw to Skinner and had left two doors unlocked to promote the escape of the two men. Card's motivation for aiding the two escapees was unclear. Before the escape, Card had a spotless record with the Sheriff's Department.

To the extent that the escape of the two men served to point out weaknesses in the county jail, it appeared that the escape did the county a favor. But the appreciation, if any, came later. For the short term, there was only embarrassment at the Sheriff's Department that the jail could be so easily broken out of by two prisoners. In the scorecard on this escape, the two escapees received much longer sentences in hard time in prison, and one deputy sheriff had his career ruined and his reputation damaged for assisting in the escape.

JIMSON WEED EXPERIMENT

Jimson weed, also known as Jamestown weed and, scientifically, as *Datura stramonium*, is a foul-smelling plant that is poisonous in every part—seed, flower and stem. It is a tall plant related to nightshade. It does produce an attractive flower. When ingested in less than fatal amounts, the plant produces hallucinogenic images. In fact, the Luiseno Indians of Southern California have been known to use jimson in initiation ceremonies to mark a youth's passage into manhood.

In the west of this country, jimson is one of those plants sometimes called "loco weed." These plants seem to drive cattle mad and are much hated by cowmen. Riverside Community College professor Cecil Johnson in the summer of 1957 decided to use himself as a human guinea pig and to take a small dose of jimson and, later, to write his impressions of the experiment for a learned journal. Before beginning the experiment, Johnson consulted with retired RCC professor Edmund Jaeger, the noted desert expert. Jaeger approved of the venture but urged Johnson to "be careful."

Johnson put some of the ground jimson into water and drank the brew. He drank no more than a few swallows of what he described as "vile-tasting brew." Soon, he found the room spinning, and he was unable to focus his eyes on anything. He could not walk or maintain balance while standing. Johnson's wife became worried when he began to stagger around and sing new songs with imaginary words. He picked bright, imaginary stars from the fabric of a couch. His dilated pupils saw super bright colors that went through the spectrum of colors. Finally, he blacked out completely.

His wife, rightly concerned, took Johnson to the Riverside County Hospital, then located at Magnolia Avenue near Harrison. The doctor on duty administered pilocarpine, an antidote for atropine poisoning. The patient suffered from both a depressed heart rate and respiratory malfunction. He was near death. Johnson found himself in a barred cell where criminals were normally placed while in the hospital. Fearing that Johnson might harm himself, workers had tied him to the bedposts of the hospital bed. His hallucinations continued.

As the effects of the drug wore off, Johnson felt extreme fatigue, probably due to his violent resisting while tied down in bed. Soon, though, he felt a strange euphoria. He felt "cleansed and pure," as he later reported. He also felt that he lived in nineteenth-century France, in a Paris inhabited by unearthly, monstrous creatures.

Professor Johnson's intent in this experiment was to advance scientific knowledge. He knew from the start that there might be unpleasant effects following the ingestion of the jimson. It should be emphasized that there was no violation of law involved in this 1957 experiment. The results of this experiment are detailed in the *International Journal of Neuropsychiatry* of June 1967. Johnson urged the reading public to avoid contact with such substances as jimson weed.

Thanks go to retired Professor Johnson, whose phone number is in the Williamsburg, Virginia directory. He has told me that he would love to hear from former colleagues and students.

For Halloween, a Ghost Mystery Is Solved

Professor Cecil Johnson was a teacher of biology at Riverside Community College for many years, and along the way, he was one of the most controversial persons ever to live in Riverside.

This writer had the privilege of chatting with Professor Johnson on the telephone. Our conversation ranged over many topics, but the most startling subject was the so-called ghost of the Santa Ana River. This ghost appeared on foggy nights in 1958–59 where North Main Street meets the Santa Ana River. The ghost appeared out of the river bottom to frighten people in cars. Those who reported seeing the creature were serious, responsible individuals. Police and press reporters responded to the scene, but no ghostly creature was ever found.

Cecil Johnson admitted to me that he was the ghost and that he enjoyed pulling off the prank on more than one occasion. He told of wearing a shiny, phosphorescent outfit and a ghostly mask. The Santa Ana River ghost was taken seriously by some, and it is mentioned in the book *Weird California* by Greg Bishop and others. This book is available at the downtown branch of the Riverside Public Library.

Cecil had a colorful career in Riverside, one that was far different from that of the typical college professor. He irritated a few people and had a fiery cross burned on his front lawn. He ran for sheriff of Riverside County against Sheriff Joe Rice, though Cecil had no previous law enforcement experience. Cecil lost that race and now admits that he would have been "a lousy sheriff." He experimented with such drugs as jimson weed and ended up in the hospital from the effects of what some have called "loco weed."

Cecil carried his controversial views and interviews to the airwaves for seven years at radio station KCKC. When Los Angeles radio personality Joe Pine went on vacation, he called on Cecil to take his place. Cecil admitted that he was once an alcoholic and that he engaged in barroom fights. He also authored seven textbooks and one article for *National Geographic*.

He now resides in Williamsburg, Virginia, a short distance from the famous Raleigh Tavern, where Jefferson and Patrick Henry met 250 years ago to plan the course of the American Revolution in Virginia. Cecil is in his mid-eighties now and is still active, alert and feisty. After retiring from RCC, he wrote a column for the *Virginia Gazette* for seven years. This is one of the oldest newspapers in the land. He also taught extension courses at the University of William and Mary.

Cecil had great fun in his role as ghost and in his many escapades that upset the establishment while creating controversy in the community. He still has both friends and enemies in Riverside, but it is unlikely that anyone ever fell asleep in any one of Cecil's classes. He was and is an unforgettable personality.

Thanks go to that veteran writer and editor Ed Mauel for his assistance on this section.

"AUDITORIUM CAN'T HOLD CROWD FOR ANN LANDERS"

These words formed the headline of a *Daily Enterprise* piece on June 11, 1959. Ann Landers was a syndicated columnist whose stock in trade was direct, and often humorous, advice to readers. She claimed to receive twenty thousand letters per month, and she swore that she answered every one of them.

Ann Landers spent a busy day in Riverside. During the school day, she spoke to assemblies at both Poly High and Ramona High School, the only two public high schools in Riverside in 1959. In the evening, she spoke to the public at the Ramona auditorium. An overflow crowd listened to a loudspeaker carry her words.

Ann Landers's visit was sponsored by the Riverside Unified School District, the Family Service Association and the *Press-Enterprise*. She was a small, energetic woman with brown hair. Her quick wit was apparent to each of her audiences.

In her daily life, Ann was Mrs. Esther Pauline Lederer, wife of a Chicago businessman. In 1959, she was the mother of a teenage daughter named Margo. Ann claimed that many of her letters came from teenagers who struggled with the usual problems of adolescence. She often referred the troubled person to local organizations such as Family Service or the Salvation Army.

Some examples of Ann Landers's wit were as follows: "Sex is here to stay" and "Sex is like dynamite. It all depends on how you use it." Referring to alcoholism, she lectured, "You can't drown your troubles in a bottle. Troubles can swim."

Ann Landers and her twin sister, who wrote a similar advice column under the name Abigail Van Buren, were daughters of Jewish immigrants who had fled tsarist Russia in 1908. The *Press-Enterprise* often ran both sisters' columns side by side. As competitors in the press, the two sisters famously did not get along. At one point, they did not speak to each other for five years.

In explaining her personal advice column, Ann Landers emphasized that her correspondents wanted answers. Indecision was a very bad solution, she concluded. In a statement, she insisted that "[m]ankind's common bond is trouble."

To assist her in providing answers, Ann Landers had a group of experts on which to call. Included in that number were U.S. Supreme Court Justice William O. Douglas and several professors of medicine. Landers's first column was printed in 1955, and she continued until her death in 2002 at age eighty-three. During her career, she wrote six books and earned thirty-three honorary degrees from various universities. She won the Albert Lasker Public Service Award for her efforts to fight cancer.

Near the end of her life, Landers maintained that "[t]he world is getting better. People are better educated. And their handwriting is easier to read."

Part IV

Late Twentieth Century

Stan Freberg and His Riverside Problems

For years, there was a huge, red letter "T" standing at the southwest corner of Arlington Avenue and Van Buren Avenue. The letter stood for Thriftimart, a large "grocery and more" chain of stores.

In January 1960, the Thriftimart store at that location had a grand opening celebration. The celebrity hired to serve as the major attraction was comedian and satirist Stan Freberg. Thriftimart promised that Freberg would be paid for his appearance with as much of the store's merchandise as he could carry out.

Stan Freberg was his usual witty self, joking and telling anecdotes to an adoring crowd. Riverside residents seemed to love Freberg and his often barbed wit. At the end of his time on stage, Freberg grabbed a market basket and began to load it with items from the store. There were two problems, neither one of the store's making. Freberg had arrived by helicopter from Los Angeles, and the pilot was pushing Freberg to hurry so the two could take off. Secondly, the helicopter had a weight limit, so Freberg had a cap on the weight of items he could take with him.

A harried and worried Stan Freberg ran around the store filling his shopping cart. "This is madness," he exclaimed. All the while the helicopter pilot was urging him, "Let's go." Thriftimart managers and employees were amused at Freberg's problems.

Freberg was born in Los Angeles and graduated from Alhambra High School. An uncle worked at Warner Bros. Studio and helped young Stan get started in show business. Stan worked as a comedy voice for movie cartoons. Satire and comedy seemed to be Freberg's major interest. He ridiculed movie westerns in "Callaway Went Thattaway" and a sobbing singer, probably Johnny Ray, in another film. He also developed a spoof of Elvis Presley.

Not everyone appreciated Freberg's satire. His recorded parody of soap operas, "John and Marsha," caused a stir. His "Green Christmas" upset retailers across the land with its criticism of materialism at Christmas. Other targets of Freberg's sharp humor included Lawrence Welk and Senator Joe McCarthy. He seemed to court controversy with his humor.

Freberg was a superior talent in many areas. At last report, he was alive at age eighty-four and living in Southern California. In his long, creative life, Freberg had few more harried times than his day in the Riverside Thriftimart in 1960.

The Hip Hypnotist

Pat Collins was a pretty blonde with an upswept hairdo of a style that was popular in the early 1960s. In 1962, Pat signed on to perform at the Dunes Nightclub in Riverside for two weekends, and she ended up performing there for seven months. As one reviewer reported, she really "packed them in" at the Dunes.

Riverside was the steppingstone to fame for the young, witty entertainer. She would hypnotize volunteers from the audience at the club, and those hypnotized would do strange, amusing things to entertain the crowd. From Riverside, Miss Collins went to Hollywood, where she appeared on Steve Allen's television program and acted in the film *Divorce American Style*. She appeared on *I Love Lucy* and became a friend of many of the Hollywood stars. Some of the stars volunteered to be hypnotized by Miss Collins. Soon, she was in demand from coast to coast. She earned $4,000 per week at the peak of her career, and that career went on for years.

In 1968, she was back in Riverside, a city she felt close to because she felt it had given her a start in show business. She performed at the Diamond Lil Nightclub, then located in the Loring Building at Seventh Street (today's Mission Inn Avenue) and Main Street. Owners of the club took advantage of Collins's fame by charging an admission price to enter the club where no such admission price had been levied before.

Imitators came to the entertainment world, some of them attractive blondes, with acts that were remarkably similar to that of Pat Collins. When asked about her imitators, Pat replied that imitation was assurance that her act was a success.

A psychotherapist interviewed for this section stated that if a therapist hypnotized a person for entertainment value, that act would be considered unethical conduct. Still, there are even today hypnotists who entertain audiences by hypnotizing volunteers. Some hypnotists appear at school assembly programs. However, hypnosis for entertainment seems to be far less common than in the heyday of Pat Collins. It appears that there are no hypnosis headliners today of the fame held by Pat Collins in the 1960s. She was one of a kind. She combined beauty, talent and wit with the ability to hypnotize a volunteer with entertaining results.

Pat Collins performed in Las Vegas and Lake Tahoe clubs and on college campuses. She attracted large crowds and media attention wherever she appeared. She did not have good health. She first encountered hypnosis when she suffered from a nervous breakdown, and she felt that hypnosis had helped in her recovery. She then went on to develop her stage act based on the process.

Years later, she suffered a stroke from which she never fully recovered. She died in New York City at age sixty-two in June 1997. Many long-term Riverside residents will remember Pat Collins from her days performing here in 1962 and 1968.

BAD DAY AT THE BALLPARK

Spring is near, and the breath of springtime provokes thoughts of baseball. For many years, baseball at all levels was played at Evans Park, then located behind the Calvary Presbyterian Church between Magnolia and Brockton Avenues. Evans Park was the spring training base for the Portland Beavers of the Pacific Coast League in the late 1940s and was the home of Riverside's minor-league professional teams, the Riverside Dons and later the Rubes, from 1947 until some time in the early 1950s.

In the spring of 1963, Evans Park was the home of the Riverside Community College baseball team. In April that year, RCC was playing against the Citrus College team of Glendora when a huge, eighty-year-old cottonwood tree situated on the property of the Calvary Presbyterian Church became uprooted and fell into the bleachers of the ballpark.

Four spectators were injured, including Jimmy Sakaguchi, father of the RCC pitcher on the mound for the home team. Vic Sakaguchi was assured that his father's injuries were minor, so he continued to pitch for his team. Injuries to one's father would unnerve most athletes, but not the young RCC pitcher. Vic continued to pitch, allowing only four hits as he and his RCC teammates defeated Citrus, 1–0, in eleven innings. The young pitcher demonstrated a concentration and determination under trying circumstances that would have been a credit to a seasoned professional pitcher.

In the bleachers, seated near the pitcher's father, was Earl McDermott, longtime history professor at RCC. He suffered only minor injuries, mostly scratches. Others slightly injured by the falling tree were Juanita Aguilera and Dick H. Fujimoto. There were very few fans in the ballpark that spring day at Evans Park. Had the stands been filled, many more injuries would have resulted from the sudden, unexpected crash of the falling tree. Some time later, the aged Evans Park was demolished—a demolition that one might say began with the crash of the tree. An office building is on the site today.

Vic Sakaguchi operates a gardening business in Riverside today. McDermott Hall on the RCC campus was named in honor of the late Professor Earl McDermott.

An old baseball fan once wrote that when you go to the ballpark on a warm afternoon, you may enjoy little more than time in the sun. Or, you may see a close, exciting game and have a memorable day. And this fan was referring only to events on the field of play.

Tunnel Leads to Cold War Civil Defense

An urban legend maintained that tunnels began under the Landis Auditorium of Riverside Community College (RCC) leading all the way to downtown. Eager to find the truth, I met with RCC president Tom Harris and Landis Auditorium supervisor Jodi Julian. We entered the basement of the auditorium and moved two heavy metal doors. Behind the doors, there was an area of ten feet by fifty feet, and off this area were three openings that looked like tunnels, but they were filled with dirt.

Jerry Longman and Raymond Couture, two Landis Auditorium workers, informed us that the tunnels are purely for utility purposes and that they end under the rear seats of the auditorium. We were disappointed in the tunnels, but the ten-by-fifty room where we stood had some most noteworthy items. The room was used as a storage area for civil defense supplies from the days of the Cold War. There were packages of biscuits dated 1963. Drums of water stored there, no longer fresh, came from the same period. The phrase "civil defense" is seldom used now, since there is little fear of an atomic attack, but rogue nations and terrorist actions could bring the term back. The phrases "emergency management" and "disaster preparedness" are generally used today. In the years from the 1950s to the 1970s, Riverside County had several civil defense directors. They were generally retired military officers, and they included Mel Stark and Bob Harrigan.

Patty and Leon Spaugy, retired County of Riverside employees, told me that tunnels exist between the County Administrative Building on Lemon Street and the sheriff's headquarters on Orange Street. In addition, they informed me that the basement of the administration building contains, again behind heavy steel doors, stored supplies similar to those found at Landis Auditorium.

In addition, there are showers in that basement shelter so that victims of an atomic attack could wash off the radioactive dust. The statements of Mr. and Mrs. Spaugy were confirmed by two Riverside County officials, Tom Freeman and Peter Lent. Lent added that one half of the cost of the tunnels, supplies and equipment was paid for by the Federal Emergency Management Administration (FEMA). The building and tunnel were built in the mid-1960s, Lent told me.

The City of Riverside also maintains a disaster preparedness office headed by Anthony Coletta, a former Indio firefighter. His primary concern is the likelihood of a major earthquake, but disasters may take many forms. It should be heartening to the public that there are local officials, city and county, who are planning and preparing for possible disasters that we all hope never come. Japan's recent tsunami and nuclear experiences shows that shocking disasters may arrive in multiple forms.

Escaped Snake Caused Fear, Panic

It was November 1963, a few days before the shocking death of President John F. Kennedy, when a snake escaped from its confinement and disappeared behind filing cabinets in the Riverside Metropolitan Museum building at the corner of Mission Inn Avenue and Orange Street.

At that time, the building was shared by the Riverside Police Department and the museum. This must have been an uneasy relationship at best, particularly when an escaped snake struck fear in the hearts of employees and visitors. Possibly even inmates in the jail located within the building were made uncomfortable when they learned of the elusive, slithering snake at large in the building.

City museum employee Ron Pidot conducted classes for children on the second floor of the museum. He had a snake that he kept in a glass cage. He had placed heavy books on top of the cage to confine it. Pidot admits that he underestimated the strength of the snake. It was able to force the books aside and escape. A police department records clerk named Mrs. Waynedoll Bird encountered the snake in the hallway, but the snake scurried behind some filing cabinets. The reptile was loose in the city building for two weeks before being recaptured and confined by Ron Pidot.

The headline in the *Riverside Daily Press* of November 19, 1963, read, "Police Solve a Slippery Problem at Headquarters."

Ron Pidot, who now lives in retirement in the Gavilan Hills, assured me that the escaped snake was not venomous and not dangerous. It was a California king snake. This type of snake frequently attacks and kills rattlesnakes, Ron told me. Venomous or not, snakes generally cause fear and revulsion among the public. In preparation for this section, I consulted with two professional men, a psychologist and a physician. My question was the same to each: "Do you believe that fear of snakes is inborn in humans?" The psychologist believed that all primates, including humans, are born with fear of snakes. The physician disagreed, pointing out that infants show no fear of snakes.

This snake story will remind readers of another snake escape, one that was potentially far more deadly. The story hit the headlines on April 1, 2011. Since that was April Fools' Day, many people refused to believe the story, but it was true. An Egyptian cobra had escaped from its enclosure in the Bronx Zoo in New York City. The venomous African snake was recaptured six days after its escape, and all of New York City breathed a little more easily.

The 2006 thriller film *Snakes on a Plane*, starring Samuel L. Jackson and Julianna Margulies, capitalized on the very common fear of snakes.

JOE AGUILAR HAD MANY SUCCESSES

Joe Aguilar was my friend. We first met in 1951 when he was a student at Riverside's St. Francis DeSales High School. Joe and I attended Riverside Community College together, and later, we were both members of the 1957 graduating class of Riverside's campus of the University of California (UCR).

Joe always promoted civil rights and equal opportunity for all. He traced his activism back to age thirteen, when he questioned some of the practices of the Roman Catholic Church (in which he was a dedicated lifetime member). Joe worked in Riverside for the State of California as a vocational counselor and in Los Angeles for the Federal Equal Opportunity Commission. He taught Spanish at Corona High School for three years.

In any position, he was outspoken in speech and in writing. He wrote frequent letters to the editor of the *P-E*. Because of his activism and his articulate presentation of the minority viewpoint, Joe Aguilar became a community leader. He spoke for Riverside's East Side as few others did.

As an educated and outspoken Mexican American, Joe made a few enemies, but he also gained great support. He ran for the Riverside Community College Board of Trustees in 1964 and was elected. He served two terms in that post. Later, he was defeated in his bid for the Riverside City Council.

In 1970, Joe established a restaurant, Joe Aguilar's Templo del Sol, which continues to operate on University Avenue near Iowa Avenue. That restaurant was the first of several owned by Joe and his family.

Joe always had health problems, or so it seemed. He had a kidney stone that was intensely painful. The stone was removed, and Joe used it as a paperweight and conversation piece when he worked in the Employment Department.

He never forgot that his father was limited to seating in the segregated balcony of the Fox Riverside Theater in the mid-1930s because of his Mexican ancestry. In every position he held, Joe always promoted racial and ethnic equality. He was determined to succeed through education and hard work. He not only established a successful business that still operates, but he also secured election to a post that had previously been held almost exclusively by white Anglos.

Joe Aguilar died in August 1990 at age fifty-five. He left his continuing business in the hands of his widow, Josie, and their four sons. In addition, Joe was an inspiration to many who had felt downtrodden in society. Former mayor Abner Brown, who had served with Joe on the RCC Board, described him as a "tremendous human being." A memorial scholarship has been established in Joe Aguilar's name at Riverside Community College.

The Marriage King

Glynn "Scotty" Wolfe was a Baptist minister and a hotel keeper who went through the marriage ceremony at least twenty-nine different times; he is in the *Guinness Book of World Records* for the largest number of monogamous marriages. The number twenty-nine, though, may be on the low side. A woman named Bonnie Lee Bakley claimed to be a wife whose name was overlooked in the listing of twenty-nine marriages.

Wolfe owned a run-down hotel in Blythe, on the Colorado River border with Arizona. He had well-publicized disputes with Blythe city authorities, who charged that Wolfe's hotel, the Viking Rooms on Blythe's Main Street, was a dangerous fire hazard. In reply, Wolfe stated, "This whole town is a dump." He felt that city authorities were singling him out because of his marriages and the resultant notoriety.

Wolfe's first marriage took place in 1926 and ended with the bride dying the next year. His brides seldom stayed married to Wolfe for long, though wife number twenty-eight stayed married to him for more than ten years before the divorce. After marriage to three particular women ended in divorce, he married each of these women a second time.

Several of his wives died, but most of his wives had their marriages ended by divorce. His final marriage lasted only a few months, and some thought that the marriage was no more than a publicity stunt since the bride left Wolfe after only a week of marriage to return to her Indiana home.

What kind of man was Wolfe? He was a generous Baptist minister who housed in his hotel derelicts whom no one else in town would shelter. He felt that there was some good in everyone, whether he or she be an ex-convict or a dope addict. Wolfe also fought stubbornly against the City of Blythe, which wanted to either bring Wolfe's hotel up to code or demolish it. City code officials cited blocked windows and exposed electrical wiring. They regarded the place as unsafe for human habitation.

Eventually, Reverend Glynn "Scotty" Wolfe died alone and far from his hotel in Blythe. He passed away in June 1977 in Redlands, California. It is unlikely that Wolfe set out to score a record number of marriages. It seems that things simply worked out that way.

Wolfe is no doubt remembered with mixed feelings by old-time residents of Blythe. Perhaps he was simply not understood by his brides and not tolerated by the city.

PASTOR MOSS LED THE BLACK COMMUNITY

Reverent Leander B. Moss was a spokesperson for the African American community in Riverside. *Courtesy of Riverside Metropolitan Museum.*

Leander B. Moss was born in western Texas in 1898. Early in life, he received a double call. He was called to the ministry and also called to lead the black people of the land. He became Reverend Moss and accepted the pastorate of the Park Avenue Baptist Church of Riverside on October 1, 1929. He served the church on East Side of Riverside through the Great Depression and World War II and also through times of prosperity. Moss lived in Riverside for fifty-seven years.

Moss was more than the leader of his church and more than a leader of the black community. He was a civic leader in Riverside. Moss served for years on the city's library board, during the years when censorship, expansion of library services and construction of new library buildings were important issues.

During World War II, Moss served as an air raid warden. He served for seven years as president of Riverside's chapter of the National Association for the Advancement of Colored People (NAACP). Moss was a charter member and teacher in the Providence Baptist Theological Seminary of Los Angeles. He also taught at an extension of the American Baptist Theological Seminary of Nashville, Tennessee. He found time to write and publish a book, *Romance of the California State Baptist Convention, Inc.*

Moss was disturbed by the cramped quarters of the church on Park Avenue. He led and organized a move to build a new and much larger church. The church acquired land on Pennsylvania Avenue, now Martin Luther King Jr. Boulevard. In 1980, a groundbreaking ceremony was held at the 4.5-acre site. Moss overcame financial hardships and work stoppages, and on July 8, 1984, the congregation moved from Park Avenue to the newly completed church.

Moss was proud to see the church's new home. On May 6, 1986, he passed away after fifty-seven years as the pastor of his church, his people and his city, Riverside.

Homecoming Queens of the 1960s

With the thought of a lighthearted summertime story in mind, I want to tell you about the various homecoming queens from RCC in the years from 1961 to 1967, inclusive. The yearbooks of Riverside Community College (the *Tequesquite*) from 1968 and 1969 were not available.

Which of these lovely young ladies was the most beautiful? A jury of five men was put together at the American Legion Post No. 289 on Buchanan Avenue where Riverside meets Corona. Most men were eager to judge pretty girls, even those from almost fifty years ago, but one man declined. We presume he had had a hard day on the job and was reluctant to make a decision, or any kind of decision.

Jurors included Jim "Jimbob" Thompson, Post No. 289 commander. He has some experience with beauty queens, since his wife, Patsy, is the former Miss Indiana of the 1958 All-States Picnic held on Euclid Avenue in Ontario. Brian Draper is one of the top pool players at Post No. 289, and he is known for his sharp eye. He was eager to be on the jury. Lu Rodriguez is known for his hard work in front of a hot grill. He often cooks the steaks on the Thursday steak night at the Legion post. Gorman Brown and Robert Rodriguez rounded out the five judges. All of the men took the task seriously. In fact, this group was as committed as any jury to be found in the downtown courthouse.

Joy Defenbaugh won the unofficial beauty contest held at the American Legion Post 289 in Riverside's Fairmount Park. Ms. Defenbaugh served on the Riverside City Council from 1992 to 2004. From the yearbook *Tequesquite*. *Courtesy of Riverside Community College.*

The homecoming queens were listed by year: 1961, Vicki Hughes; 1962, Marian Gross; 1963, Vicki Dow; 1964, Andrea Balogh; 1965, Joy Defenbaugh; 1966, Pat Hanson; and 1967, Cheryl Metcalf.

Each of the judges considered himself to be a true arbiter of female beauty, but even the age at which a woman reaches her peak of physical beauty was in dispute. Some accept "sweet sixteen," while others prefer the more mature woman of twenty or twenty-one.

There was no majority vote in this contest. We had to settle for a plurality from the jurors. Miss Joy Defenbaugh was the only contestant to win two first-place votes from the five judges. Therefore, we named her as the fairest of the fair. Andrea Balogh of 1964 won three votes for second place. By some measurements, that would place her ahead of Defenbaugh. Third place had to go to Pat Hanson of 1966. She won a first-place vote and a third-place vote.

No doubt there are some readers who feel that this was a stupid exercise, and who cares, anyway? The jury and I would dispute that charge. An old song proclaims, "A pretty girl is like a melody," and many women, like melodies, are unforgettable. These young women were all honored in their years at RCC, and most would be pleased to be remembered after all these years.

Which one was the most beautiful of these lovely young women? We hope we have not made one woman ecstatic and six women disappointed. That would not be reasonable. Each woman was a real beauty in her time. Thanks to all of the jurors and the supporters of this retrospective beauty contest at American Legion Post No. 289 of Riverside.

Jack Benny in Riverside

Jack Benny was possibly the most popular entertainer of his time. The public followed him from vaudeville to radio to film and on to television. In many ways, the real-life Jack Benny was the opposite of the Benny who appeared on radio or television. He was portrayed as a tightwad when, in fact, his generosity to charity was well known. He was seen as vain, but in real life, he was modest, giving his gag writers credit for his show's popularity.

In his comic routines, he had a Maxwell auto out of the 1920s, but in real life, he drove a late-model luxury sedan to Palm Springs every winter. In his act, he was a mediocre violinist. In actuality, he performed serious violin solos with major orchestras of the world.

It was the charitable Jack Benny who came to Riverside in December 1968 to perform with the Riverside Symphony Orchestra and to help the orchestra erase its accumulated debt. He donated his time and talent for a concert that became a sellout in the downtown Riverside Municipal Auditorium. In cooperation with conductor James K. Guthrie of San Bernardino, Benny offered comedy and music as he performed, as soloist, a popular Mendelssohn violin concerto.

In describing both rehearsal and performance, *Riverside Daily Press* writer T.E. Foreman repeatedly used the word "happy." Conductor, musicians and Jack Benny were all happy to be doing the benefit concert. Benny had done similar concerts for orchestras all over the nation. A concert in Oakland to benefit the local symphony orchestra had some seats that sold for $1,000 each. In the Riverside concert, the top ticket price was $100, with most seats going for $5 to $10. For $100, the Riverside concertgoer was able to attend a champagne reception with Benny after the concert.

For music purists, it was almost a sin to interrupt the Mendelssohn Violin Concerto in E minor, Op. 64, with intentional sour notes and amusing comments, but for most of the crowd, it was hilarious. Afterward, Benny complimented the Riverside audience by saying, "They laugh at everything." Benny added that the event had been one of the most pleasant of the many benefit concerts he had given over the previous eleven years.

The packed auditorium and happy music-lovers produced a net profit of $17,000 for the Riverside Symphony Orchestra. That amount was more than enough to wipe out the orchestra's debt and also provide seed money for future concerts. The evening performance was a huge success and almost a mutual love affair. Riversiders loved Jack Benny, and Benny seemed to love and admire the conductor, the musicians and the Riverside audience.

Jack Benny died in December 1974 at age eighty, six years and a few days after his Riverside concert success.

DOM FELICETTA'S MUSICAL LIFE

Dominick Felicetta came from a musical family. His father performed on the radio as a solo mandolin player in Minneapolis, where his son was born in 1935. The family moved to Riverside in part because the area reminded Dom's father of his native Italy.

In Riverside, the family opened Felicetta's Shoe Repair Shop, and young Dom shined shoes there after school and on Saturdays in order to earn spending money. Dom chose the stand-up bass as his instrument of choice. He played in the band under the direction of the late Lester Oaks at Poly High and went on to study music for two years at Riverside Community College. Along the way, Dom played at local nightclubs that only old-timers will remember. Included were the Alpine Club of Colton and the Banker's Club of San Bernardino. One night, he was playing as part of a group in the House of Norman in Rialto when a pretty girl named Louise walked in. Dom was taken with her, and they were married a few months later.

Dom auditioned for the Lawrence Welk Orchestra but was rejected, not because of his musical performance but because he was not married at the time. The Welk organization insisted on married musicians because the management felt that married people were more stable than single ones.

Dom was hired to be part of the Perez Prado Band, a group that specialized in Cuban Latin music. The group had several big hits in the 1950s and 1960s and traveled the country to perform before thousands of admiring fans. Life on the road gets tiring, even when one is part of a highly paid and popular group. Dom returned to Riverside, where he performed at local clubs as part of such groups as the Swinging Safari. He also helped his aging father in the shoe repair shop.

Dom grew beyond being a performer. He often served as master of ceremonies. He even sang and told jokes. He was popular with the crowds wherever he went. Dom also always kept up with his high school friends, so it was natural that they chose him to be master of ceremonies at the Poly High School reunion for the fiftieth anniversary of the class of 1953. Dom wore a tuxedo and gave a professional performance to his amused and admiring classmates of fifty years before.

Dom became suddenly ill and died on January 20, 2007. His high school class holds an annual picnic each June in Fairmount Park. Dom was honored there by a jazz group and by a flyover of airplanes, organized by Dom's friend and classmate Dennis Timmons. It was a fitting tribute to a talented and gracious man.

The Felicetta family shoe repair shop still operates as Tom's Shoe Repair in Riverside's Brockton Arcade. Dom left a widow and four children, eight grandchildren and two great-grandchildren. The headline over his long obituary in the *San Bernardino Sun* read, "Musician Was Able to Light Up a Room."

PATRICIA BEATTY LEFT HER MARK

Patricia Beatty, born in 1922, was a graduate of Reed College in Oregon and came to Riverside as a faculty wife. Her husband, John Beatty, was a history professor who was part of the original faculty of the College of Arts and Sciences of Riverside's campus of the University of California–Riverside.

Pat and the professor had a daughter, but still the energetic Mrs. Beatty wanted an active life outside the home. She became a reference librarian at the downtown Riverside Public Library. She was remembered for her determined stride and for her lack of patience with those who asked foolish questions. She was serious and resolute, and she expected others to be the same.

While working at the library, she became interested in writing stories. That interest became almost an obsession. There were several reasons for her amazing productivity as an author. In addition to innate intelligence, she had a fine educational background. Finally, she was able to get by on very little sleep; she often wrote in the quiet hours from 10:00 p.m. until 2:00 a.m. The result was a total of fifty books, mostly written for children, and numerous articles. Possibly the most famous of her books, *The Queen's Own Grove*, is set in the Riverside of the 1880s.

A former Riverside librarian, Patricia Beatty wrote more than fifty historical children's novels during the quiet hours of 10:00 p.m. and 2:00 a.m. *Courtesy of Patricia Beatty Elementary School.*

Pat was an active member of the Zonta Club and the National Organization for Women. She participated in UCR faculty activities with her husband, a professor most called Jack. Pat often expressed a grim view of life, as did some other writers, including Mark

Riverside Unified School District opened Patricia Beatty Elementary School in 2007 on Latham Street in Riverside. *Courtesy of Patricia Beatty Elementary School.*

Twain. She told an interviewer, "Smiles and laughter are not luxuries but real necessities to lighten the load of life."

Pat's 1972 book *Lupita Mañana* won the Jane Addams Children's Book Award. Former head Riverside librarian Judith Auth had high praise for the writer: "Pat had a gift not only for the history and the drama, but for the real emotions of real people."

After the death of Professor Jack Beatty, Pat married another UC Riverside faculty member, economics professor Carl G. Uhr. Pat Beatty died in July 1991 at age sixty-nine.

The Riverside Unified School District honored Pat Beatty by naming a new elementary school for her. It opened in 2008 and is a showplace school, modern and beautiful in every respect. The 740-student school is on a ten-acre campus on Latham Street north of Fairmount Park. The students are known as the Beatty Bobcats, and their slogan is "I am the author of my future," appropriate words for students of a school named for a highly respected Riverside author.

NEW FIRE STATION ON SITE OF EMBARRASSMENT

Until recently, a large, multicolored sign stood on the northwest corner of University Avenue and Lime Street in downtown Riverside. The sign announced the city's intention to construct a new, large central fire station on that lot, a lot now used for parking. The sign is gone now. Councilman Mike Gardner told me that the sign was taken down because it was about to fall down. Though the sign is gone, the plans for the new fire station remain in place. There is only one problem: funding. The city hopes to receive federal grants that will fund all or part of the construction, according to Councilman Gardner.

That vacant lot where the sign stood has quite a past. In the 1880s, a four-story hotel with eighty rooms and twenty-three baths was built there. For a few years, it housed the County of Riverside offices. As a hotel, it

Some felt that the old Tetley or Riverside Hotel was ready for demolition before a fire destroyed it, producing heavy criticism for the Riverside Fire Department next door. *Courtesy of Riverside Metropolitan Museum.*

had various names through its long history. Included among them were the Arlington Hotel, the Tetley Hotel and the Riverside Hotel.

In the 1960s, the present downtown fire station was constructed right across the alley from the old hotel, a structure by this time quite run down and home to mostly elderly pensioners. Then, in 1973, the ancient hotel caught fire. Its old, dry wood burned rapidly. The firemen located across the alley from the burning structure did not have the equipment to reach the top floors of the building.

Fire trucks and firemen were called in from several nearby cities, and the firefighters fought the blaze valiantly, but to no avail. The structure burned to the ground and was a total loss. Naturally, the city council and the public had some questions. Why couldn't Riverside's fire department, located right across the alley from the blaze, put out the fire promptly? Some citizens were indignant. "We are paying for that fire department!" they exclaimed.

An investigation was held, and it was found that Riverside had been buying cheap, ineffective fire engines. Provisions had not been made for a high-rise fire. Charges and countercharges were made, along with excuses and explanations. In the end, it was a great embarrassment for the Riverside Fire Department. Some citizens pointed out that firemen could almost spit across the alley to the flames that engulfed the old hotel building. The cause of the fire was thought to be either a misplaced cigarette or a hotel guest's hotplate. The small fire became a big blaze when the frightened guest ran away from it.

The destruction of the large hotel had implications far beyond the block that contained both hotel and fire station. Fire insurance rates are based, in part, on the presence or absence of an effective fire department in the area.

Now back to the sign that has been removed. One of the rooms in the proposed new fire station to be built—ironically on the site of the 1973 hotel fire—will be a Riverside Fire Department Museum, according to that sign. This observer is eager to see how the museum describes that destructive fire that took place right across the alley from the city's main fire station.

Insane Maybe, Athletic Certainly

David Richard Campbell, age thirty-eight, was in the Riverside County Jail then located on top of the courthouse building at Eleventh and Orange Streets. Yes, Riverside County once had a penthouse jail. In January 1983, Campbell made a daring escape. Campbell was in custody and facing a murder charge of an Orange County man. He was a suspect in two other killings.

Campbell appeared before Judge Ernest M. Lopez and answered the charges against him by pleading not guilty by reason of insanity. Judge Lopez ordered psychiatric examination of the accused man. While awaiting the results of the doctors' findings, Campbell escaped.

The accused man took advantage of an argument involving other prisoners that distracted the guard at the fourth-floor rooftop outdoor exercise yard. While the guard was preoccupied, Campbell unhooked the wire mesh, slid through the opening and jumped to a ledge below. From there, he jumped onto a tall, thin *Washingtonia robusta* palm tree and slid four floors to the ground. Still in prison clothing, he made his escape. Sheriff's helicopters and police in cars and on the ground could not catch up with the escapee.

Less than twenty-four hours later, a motorist saw a suspicious person huddled near a residential wall. It was Campbell. He had stolen clothing from a Goodwill donation bin and had disposed of his prison uniform. When a policeman approached the man, the cop asked, "What is your name?" The escapee answered correctly, "Campbell." He was returned to the county jail with an additional charge of escape on his record. He told the arresting officers that he would be better off in jail, especially since he had suffered numerous cuts and a serious groin injury when he shimmied down the tall palm tree to the ground.

Authorities reviewed the escape, and some wanted to cut down the tall palm tree that Campbell had used to make his escape. Tree lovers and others objected to the planned removal of the tree. Why blame the tree, they argued, for a most unusual escape, an escape method that was not likely to happen again? *Press-Enterprise* columnist Dan Bernstein defended the palm tree, stating that if the tree had been planted by Frank Miller of Mission Inn fame, it would have been named a city monument.

Today, it is almost thirty years after the Campbell escape. The jail is no longer on top of the county courthouse. Instead, the jail is in a much larger structure at the corner of Tenth and Orange Streets. The tall feather duster palm tree used by Campbell in his escape is still there. Campbell's insanity claim was apparently rejected. He was sentenced to prison in 1991 for life without possibility of parole.

It is most unusual that a man who claimed to be insane could carry out such a daring, athletic escape while under guard. Campbell denied that fellow prisoners had staged a distraction in order to assist his escape, but law enforcement people did not believe this disclaimer.

The *Mona Lisa* of America

No one can fully explain why the painting *American Gothic* so completely captured the imagination of the public. Was it the rural setting with the plain farm home? Was it the rustic dress of the man with the pitchfork and the woman with the severe expression and the homemade dress? Or was it the totality of the persons shown plus the farmhouse background?

In any case, the 1930 painting has been reproduced hundreds of times, often with different faces shown in cartoons or parodies. Grant Wood was a midwestern painter born in 1900. He painted his sister and his family's dentist standing in front of a carpenter Gothic farmhouse in Eldon, Iowa. The house still stands and is a tourist attraction today.

Grant Wood's sister, Nan Wood, was his second choice for the female subject in the painting. Initially, Grant felt that Nan's face was too fat for his purposes. A spinster living nearby was his first choice for the role. In the end, Wood slimmed down Nan's face in the painting and gave her the severe, somewhat blank expression that has caused some critics to compare Nan's image in the painting to the *Mona Lisa* by Leonardo da Vinci.

Nan Wood married a salesman named Emmett Graham, and the couple moved frequently, sixteen times within Los Angeles alone. They had no children. Finally, they decided to move to Riverside, and Nan and her husband agreed that this move would be their last. They lived in a house on Verde Street less than one block from Ramona High School.

In 1986, Emmett died, and Nan Wood Graham lived in the Verde Street house until 1985, when she decided to move in with her friend from childhood in Menlo Park, California. Nan's health worsened, and she moved across the street into a nursing home, where she died at age ninety-one in December 1990.

During her years in Riverside, Nan was amazed at the many times *American Gothic* was depicted, distorted and misused for advertising or political purposes. She accepted most of the depictions, but sometimes she felt that her image had been maliciously misused. She sued *Playboy* and *Look* magazines, and the case were settled out of court. One of her reactions to the prominence of the painting was, "Grant made a personality out of me. I would have had a very drab life without it." Nan insisted that the painting was not a critical or sarcastic view of rural life. She claimed that her brother's only critical painting was the painting of the Daughters of the Revolution.

Grant Wood never married and died at age fifty-one in 1942. Wood was never able to explain the popularity, if that is the word, of *American Gothic.* He was saddened by the many people in Iowa who resented the painting and claimed that it was unrealistic. One critic charged that Nan Wood's mysterious expression in the painting "would curdle milk." The critic later regretted that harsh comment.

Almost everyone who looks at the painting assumes that it shows a farmer and his wife. But it could be a farmer and his daughter.

GREGORY PECK VISITED A MOVAL SCHOOL

Many actors and other celebrities promote worthwhile causes—groups, anti-disease movements and so on. Jerry Lewis has his multiple sclerosis crusade, and Bono works to reduce AIDS in Africa. The legendary Hollywood actor Gregory Peck had several causes, but one of his more modest associations involved public school classes in Moreno Valley.

Gregory Peck starred in such different films as *Gentlemen's Agreement* in 1948 and *MacArthur* in 1977. In the middle of his career, in 1962, Peck starred as Atticus Finch in *To Kill a Mockingbird.* This film was based on the novel by Harper Lee, and the film won Gregory Peck the Oscar for "Best Actor" that year. The novel was and is popular reading in intermediate school and high school classes. One of those teachers, Christine Reifel, while teaching the novel in Alessandro Middle School in 1986, had her students write to Gregory Peck to invite him to visit their classroom in Moreno Valley.

Peck accepted the invitation and passed around to the students the Oscar statuette he had won and the script for *Mockingbird.* He claimed that the Atticus Finch role in that film was his favorite of all the roles he had played in his fifty-year acting career. Peck visited Ms. Reifel's classes twice, once in 1986 and again in 1990. He claimed that he got more out of visiting the Moreno Valley school than his listeners did. Students first read the novel and then saw the movie based on it. Finally, the star of the film appeared to discuss the story with the students. They were thrilled to have such a prominent Hollywood celebrity visit their classroom.

For his part, Peck was pleased to meet the students and learn their views of the film and the novel. Students, teacher and actor agreed that the story of *Mockingbird* was a tale that will endure, a story that touches lasting human concerns and emotions.

Gregory Peck was a versatile actor who portrayed soldiers in combat, Abraham Lincoln, Captain Ahab in *Moby Dick* and a wild cowboy in *Duel in the Sun*. Early in Peck's career, his role in *Gentlemen's Agreement* was a pioneering role in dealing with discrimination, in that case anti-Semitism. That movie won the Oscar for best film of 1948.

Christine Reifel, the host teacher, admires Peck greatly. She concluded that "[h]e lived his life in the fight against ignorance and prejudice." Ms. Reifel still lives in Riverside. One of the lessons the students learned was that Peck was a real flesh-and-blood human being who was not the same as the character he played in the film. He was an actor playing a role, one that students could sympathize with, but an actor nonetheless.

A postage stamp commemorated the career of Gregory Peck, a favorite of students and a teacher in Moreno Valley. *Courtesy of U.S. Postal Service.*

Peck's final role was in *The Portrait* with Lauren Bacall in 1993. He died in 2003 at age eighty-seven. My film guide lists Peck's credits as forty-seven films stretching from 1943 to 1993.

NORTON YOUNGLOVE: LONGTIME COUNTY SUPERVISOR

Norton Younglove was born in 1929 to a fourth-generation Riverside family. He and education leader Lew Vanderzyl are old friends who have known each other since grade school. Younglove served as Riverside County supervisor for twenty-four years, making him the third longest-serving member of that county government body. He is still active and well and living on Hawarden Drive in Riverside.

In a March 1990 evaluation of the members of the board of supervisors, the *Press-Enterprise* rated Younglove number one in his understanding of regional, state and federal issues. Inevitably, in public life, Younglove received criticism as well as compliments. More than one critic charged that he was the captive of the developers. Yet he pushed for, and achieved, a fee placed on new developments to benefit parks and other county projects.

His constituents often praised his intelligence and humane nature. He represented the areas of Highgrove, Moreno Valley and Perris in the period of those areas' greatest growths.

One of the strangest attacks made on Younglove was a personal one. Ruth Russo, who opposed him for reelection in 1990, charged that Younglove was an alcoholic. She offered no evidence of a drunk-driving charge or other alcohol-influenced misbehavior. The voters of the Fifth District responded by reelecting Younglove to a sixth term as supervisor, with 58.6 percent of the vote. Ruth Russo received 25.7 percent, and a third candidate, Ken Skinner, received 15.4 percent. In supporting Younglove's bid for a sixth term, they were voting for his experience and were reaffirming the code of the Old West. That code held that no person should criticize a man's drinking habits so long as the drinker behaves himself.

A more serious charge against Younglove was the nondisclosure of campaign donations that resulted in a fine of $7,500 in 1990. He insisted that the omission was a mere clerical error and that he had always intended to comply with all requirements of the law.

Leon Spaugy served the County of Riverside as agricultural commissioner and director of weights and measures. He noted that Supervisor Younglove was "always available" and that he was "astute and businesslike." Spaugy added that with Younglove an employee had to be prepared. "Sometimes he would challenge assertions, and if you had no support for your claim, he would vote against it." Retired judge John Gabbert was pleased to recall running into Mr. and Mrs. Younglove on a Rhine cruise in Germany. Neither official knew that the other would be there.

In September 1993, Supervisor Younglove announced that he would not seek reelection in June 1994. He told the press that he was "tired of the 60 to 80 hour work weeks." When asked to name his proudest accomplishments in government, Younglove cited his efforts to secure Box Springs Mountain Park for the county, the community centers in Mead Valley and Calimesa and the imposition of developer fees. He was also proud of his service on the Air Quality Management District, which managed to reduce air pollution in our area.

Few officials of government, at any level, have influenced the development of western Riverside County as much as Supervisor Norton Younglove.

Party Held at the Italian Garden

As mentioned earlier, a wonderful evening was had at the Policemen's Ball held in downtown Riverside's Municipal Auditorium in 1949, and the cost for the evening—with two bands, a magician and the "King of the Banjo," Riverside resident Eddie Peabody—was just one dollar. Prices were lower in 1949. Let me describe a party that I wish I had attended. You or I could have gone to this party for an admission charge of thirty-five dollars, which would have benefited the Riverside Art Museum.

The afternoon-evening party was held in September 1992 on the multi-acre estate of Tom and Barbara Mazzetti on Grace Street in the Victoria area. Tom and Barbara, the former Barbara Sprague, are civic-minded residents who graduated from Poly High School in the mid-1950s. Tom manages the Blue Banner citrus packinghouse on Third Street in Riverside.

The theme of the 1992 party was Italian, and Tom is of Italian descent. The patio and garden were decorated in the colors of the Italian flag—red, white, and green. The Mazzetti estate contains more than one hundred trees and dozens of bushes in several distinct gardens. A full-time gardener kept the grounds in shape back in 1992. At the party, a tenor and a soprano sang Italian opera songs accompanied by strolling musicians. Paintings were on display and listed for sale by artists who were present.

There was a "grape stomp" in cooperation with Don Galleano of the Galleano Winery of Mira Loma. It was just the thing to color a person's feet and legs with a rich shade of purple. It is unclear whether guests stomped the grapes or whether that task was left to the Galleano winemakers.

Food offered at the party included hors d'oeuvres, soft drinks, wine and freshly stomped grape juice, some of which would later be made into wine. There was available a sampling of Italian dishes to go with the Galleano Wine. For dessert, there was Italian-style ice cream, probably spumoni.

Guests were invited to play bocce ball, a popular Italian bowling game, and to throw horseshoes in the horseshoe pit. Some swam in the large pool that adjoins a gazebo and a memorial topiary, which is shaped like the peacock whose call was well known in the neighborhood. Persons in attendance could use the Jacuzzi and waterfall under the stony gaze of a statue of cupid.

The Mazzetti family certainly knew how to throw a luxurious party, with its many varied sights and activities on their beautiful estate. For those who attended, the party was no doubt unforgettable. Wouldn't it be wonderful if the Mazzettis were to throw a "Repeat Italian Party" to duplicate the 1992 event? If such a benefit party were held in the near future, I would be near the head of the line to buy tickets.

Part V

Miscellany

Presidential Portraits

When a visitor walks through the lobby of the Mission Inn, probably the first thing he notices is the wide armchair built for the huge girth of President William Howard Taft. His weight was estimated to be 318 pounds, and he would not have been comfortable in an ordinary chair.

Behind the Taft chair, on the wall, are the portraits of ten former presidents of the United States who are claimed to be associated with the Mission Inn or the Glenwood Hotel, as the hotel was previously named. The first in the series of portraits is that of the bearded President Benjamin Harrison, who spoke briefly in front of the Glenwood Hotel in April 1891. He showed appreciation for the gifts of fruit and flowers presented by Allis Miller, daughter of Frank Miller, later famous as the master of the Mission Inn. After Harrison's brief talk, he hurried off to the train station for departure.

The second president claimed by the Mission Inn was William McKinley. The claim is uncertain. In the words of the portrait wall, McKinley was "believed to have visited" the Glenwood Hotel a short time before he was killed by an assassin's bullet. McKinley had passed through Redlands on the train before visiting Riverside.

President Theodore Roosevelt stayed at the Mission Inn in May 1903 and was photographed while planting a tree in the courtyard of the hotel. The rooms occupied by Roosevelt were later called the Presidential Suite and today form the Presidential Lounge, the hotel bar.

In October 1909, President William Howard Taft was honored at a banquet held in the Mission Inn, but he did not spend the night there.

Herbert Hoover stayed at the Mission Inn in the 1920s while serving as secretary of commerce and again years after leaving the White House. He had come to Riverside to confer with fellow Republicans in preparation for the 1940 election campaign.

John F. Kennedy, the only Democrat pictured on the lobby wall, was a hotel guest in December 1940, twenty years before taking office as president. Kennedy served as a reporter at the Institute of World Affairs held annually for many years at the inn.

Richard M. Nixon was married at the inn in June 1940. The room where the wedding took place is today's Presidential Lounge. Nixon's wedding reception was held in the Spanish Art Gallery. There is no evidence that the couple spent their wedding night at the inn.

Gerald Ford was a guest in the Mission Inn in March 1988, there to assist in a fundraiser for Mary Bono, a member of Congress. Ford's visit to the inn took place ten years after he had left the presidency.

Ronald Reagan married Nancy Davis in San Fernando in March 1952. The couple then spent the first night of their honeymoon in the Mission Inn. The Reagans' stay at the inn took place almost thirty years before he became president.

George W. Bush was present at a September 1999 reception hosted by the owner of the inn, Duane Roberts. He was there again in 2003 as a guest at the inn.

It appears from information provided that the only two who stayed in the Mission Inn while serving as president of the United States were Theodore Roosevelt and George W. Bush. Coincidentally, their stays were in 1903 and 2003, one hundred years apart. The other presidents pictured on the wall of the inn either failed to stay in the hotel or were guests at the inn before becoming president or after leaving office.

RIALTO TO THE NORTH

A Riverside resident may look at the city of Rialto and picture a huge funnel, wide at the north and narrow and the south, that leads to

Riverside. Indeed, the main north–south street of Rialto is Riverside Drive. It is a divided street similar to Riverside's Victoria Avenue and to parts of Magnolia Avenue. One of the founders of Rialto, a Methodist Minister named A.F. Naftzer, lived in Riverside for a time, and it is likely, but not proven, that he modeled his principal north–south street after the Riverside Avenues noted for their beauty.

Rialto was founded in 1911, and last November marked the city's centennial. It is a bedroom community of 100,000 people. Many of its residents work in Riverside and have frequent contacts with it. The trip from downtown Rialto to downtown Riverside is a mere ten miles, which makes Rialto closer to downtown Riverside than Orangecrest, a section officially within the city of Riverside.

The latest University of California–Riverside alumni directory lists 222 graduates of UCR who live in Rialto. Similar connections between Riverside and Rialto exist in many areas, though Rialto is in San Bernardino County.

Rialto has been for much of its history a citrus community, though today there is only one orange grove left in the city. It is owned by John Anthony Adams, who earned a PhD in soil science from Riverside's UCR.

The Rialto Museum displays forty-eight different citrus packinghouse labels from the city's past. My favorite is the one titled "Rialto Beauties." Those are oranges described, not pretty girls.

Geographically, Rialto is favored by an abundant water supply. It is directly south of Lytle Creek, and Rialto was first provided water by an open ditch from the creek, and later a huge pipeline carried water to thirsty citizens and to the town's orange groves.

Leaving Riverside on Main Street and heading north, one notes that Main Street becomes Riverside Avenue at the San Bernardino County line. The motorist crosses a wide, new bridge across railway yards and the Ten Freeway into Rialto, which calls itself the "Bridge City." There are two theories as to the origin of the city's name. One holds that Rialto is a contraction of Rio Alto ("high river" in Spanish). The second theory, favored by Richard McInnis of the Rialto Museum, is that the daughter of a wealthy early landowner toured Europe and visited Venice, where she was fascinated with the Rialto Bridge, a bridge so old that Shakespeare mentioned it in *Merchant of Venice*. Today, a likeness of the Venetian Rialto Bridge is featured on the city seal of Rialto.

Rialto had no more than three thousand residents in 1920. Like Riverside, Rialto grew rapidly, with subdivisions replacing orange groves in the years after World War II. Today, Rialto's biggest employer is either the local school district or the Toys "R" Us warehouse, according to Richard McInnis. It remains essentially a bedroom community, with its main street directed toward Riverside and also named for Riverside.

A trip to the Rialto Historical Museum is worthwhile for anyone interested in the development of the area. The museum is a former church building located at Riverside Avenue and Second Street. The colorful history of Rialto may be previewed in the title of John A. Adams's book, *Scammers, Schemers, and Dreamers*. I have donated my copy of this book to the Riverside Public Library, downtown branch.

CITY SLOGANS WITH A QUIZ TO FOLLOW

Most cities and towns have something to be proud of—a festival, a geographical feature or a tradition. Hinckley, Ohio, holds an annual Buzzard Festival. Sweetwater, Texas, has a Rattlesnake Festival.

Closer to home, Colton calls itself the "Hub City." Rialto has labeled itself the "Bridge City." Moreno Valley builds on the nearby the March air base by using "soar" in its tagline.

Corona has called itself the "Circle City" based on its Grand Avenue, which forms a large circle in the center of the city. Pasadena calls itself the "City of Roses." Temecula uses its historic Old Town in its official description.

The city of Banning called itself "Stagecoach City" for many years. Claremont calls itself the "City of Trees," and wags have added "and PhDs" because of the large number of professors from the city's seven colleges.

"Welcome to Glendora: Pride of the Foothills" is one city slogan represented by signage. *Photo by the author.*

Some descriptions are fanciful at best. Upland calls itself the "City of Gracious Living," as if residents in other cities live less graciously. Ontario called itself the "Balanced City" for years. Was Ontario suggesting that other cities were mentally unbalanced? Glendora proclaims that it is the "Pride of the Foothills."

Take the City Quiz

How attentive are you as you drive from city to city in inland Southern California? Some slogans are accurate, as in "Horse City, USA" for Norco. Others are less realistic, perhaps reflecting a reality from past decades.

In the quiz that follows, start by giving yourself ten points for attempting the quiz. Next, match the city at left with the description at right. Each correct answer is worth five points. The total number of correct answers times five, plus the ten bonus points, will produce the total score.

A score of one hundred points is perfect, and ninety points will merit an A grade. Answers to this quiz will appear below the quiz.

1. Temecula	A. The Hub City
2. San Bernardino	B. The Balanced City
3. Fontana	C. The Gate City
4. Riverside	D. The City of the Roses
5. Ontario	E. City of Gracious Living
6. Upland	F. The Bridge City
7. Rialto	G. The Circle City
8. Colton	H. The Fair City
9. Pomona	I. The Steel City
10. Corona	J. City of the Arts
11. Pasadena	K. Pride of the Foothills
12. Glendora	L. Horse City, USA
13. Norco	M. Stagecoach City
14. Chino	N. Canyon City
15. Banning	O. Where Everything Grows
16. Azusa	P. City of Trees (and PhDs)
17. Claremont	Q. Where Dreams Soar
18. Moreno Valley	R. Old Town, New Opportunities

(ANSWERS: 1R; 2C; 3I; 4J; 5B; 6E; 7F; 8A; 9H; 10G; 11D; 12K; 13L; 14O; 15M; 16N; 17P; 18Q)

STAR SAVED BY A DUMMY

This was my farewell column for the *Press-Enterprise*. My departure from those pages was not voluntary. I wrote the weekly local history column for seven years, some 350 columns in all. It was a great experience, and I thank the good people of Riverside and environs who helped me with suggestions and information for those columns.

Riverside has amusing historical incidents and even star-studded moments. Here is one, and as I depart I will try to leave the reader laughing, or at least smiling.

May Grow Stobbs was a judge in the Jurupa Justice Court from 1949 to 1959. At first, she was a justice of the peace, and in 1952, her title was changed to judge of the Jurupa Justice Court. By either title, Judge Stobbs was the judge for minor disputes and infractions in the area now known as Jurupa Valley.

In cooperation with her friend Mary H. Haggland and the facilities of the Jurupa Mountain Cultural Center, Judge Stobbs wrote her memoirs. While normally the law and courts are very serious subjects, Judge Stobbs recalled one most amusing incident.

Sometime in the late 1930s or early 1940s, the actress Dorothy Lamour, who was known to have a heavy foot on the gas pedal, was stopped in West Riverside (today's Rubidoux) and given a speeding ticket for going forty-seven miles per hour in a twenty-mile zone.

As Ms. Lamour proceeded through Riverside toward Palm Springs, where she was to be filmed, she was stopped for speeding a second time by another motorcycle patrolman. While the officer was talking to Ms. Lamour, a roadster came by, and what appeared to be a young male leaned out from the back seat and called the officer a "baboon." The officer was angry and promptly forgot about Ms. Lamour and the speeding ticket he intended to write. The actress drove off without the second speeding ticket.

The motorcycle patrolman took off in pursuit of the insulting youth. But this impudent person was not a youth. He was not even human. Edgar Bergen, a famous ventriloquist, was seated in the back of the roadster with his famous dummy, Charlie McCarthy. Bergen had pushed the face of his dummy out the window, and the dummy was the face the officer had seen while Bergen provided the voiced insult.

It would have been most amusing to see and hear the interaction between the officer, Bergen and the wooden dummy. As so often happens, we do not know the end of this story, except to conclude that Ms.

Lamour probably deserved two speeding tickets that day, though she received only one thanks to the intervention of Bergen and his dummy.

Dorothy Lamour appeared in fifty-five films, beginning in 1930. She starred in the "Road" series with Bing Crosby and Bob Hope. She deserved public sympathy because Hope and Crosby often played tricks on her, practical jokes that she found most annoying.

Edgar Bergen appeared in eleven films and is the father of Candice Bergen, like Ms. Lamour one of Hollywood's true beauties. Edgar died at age seventy-five in 1978. Perhaps Candice Bergen has inherited the wooden Charlie McCarthy and his country cousin, Mortimer Snerd.

Dorothy Lamour, seen here in a publicity still, was ticketed for speeding in Rubidoux. *Courtesy of Steve Takata.*

ABOUT THE AUTHOR

Harold Lee Durian was born in June 1935 in Costa Mesa, California. A few days after his birth, Howard Hughes crashed his racing monoplane a few miles from Hal's home.

The son of a U.S. Navy chief petty officer and a housewife, Hal lived in Elsinore (Lake Elsinore today), Beaumont and then Riverside. Hal attended public schools in Riverside and graduated from Poly High School in 1953 and the University of California–Riverside in 1957. He earned an MA in history from the University of Arizona in 1969.

Hal spent two years in the U.S. Naval Reserve and visited many Mediterranean ports. Upon his discharge from the navy, Hal taught history and government at Chaffey High School in Ontario for forty-one years. Hal has been married for forty-eight years to the former Barbara Anne Clarke. They have three sons.

Hal wrote a weekly column on history for the *Riverside Press-Enterprise* from July 2005 to July 2012. The Durians have traveled extensively since his retirement from teaching, to Russia, Spain, China and India. "Age is an achievement," Hal believes. "Youth is a mere accident."